SOME SLAVES

OF

WARREN COUNTY, VIRGINIA

WILL BOOKS A, B, C

1835–1904

COMPILED BY

Sandra Barlau

HERITAGE BOOKS
2024

HERITAGE BOOKS

AN IMPRINT OF HERITAGE BOOKS, INC.

Books, CDs, and more—Worldwide

For our listing of thousands of titles see our website
at
www.HeritageBooks.com

Published 2024 by
HERITAGE BOOKS, INC.
Publishing Division
5810 Ruatan Street
Berwyn Heights, MD 20740

International Standard Book Number
Paperbound: 978-0-7884-3068-8

TABLE OF CONTENTS

iv

PREFACE

The idea for the Slaves of Virginia series was conceived when I decided to find the mother of my enslaved 2nd gr-grandmother Mildred Timbers. How did Alexander Jeffries obtain her? She could have been willed (the reason for reading the Fauquier will books), deeded, gifted, or purchased.

After reading the Fauquier County, Virginia will books 1-31 from 1759 to 1869 I determined that she was not willed to him. That left the the deed books and tax records. I used the same format for the deed books as I had for the will books and set up a spreadsheet for the tax records. I included a column in the spreadsheet that added the number of slaves owned. That column was very useful because any changes in the number of slaves each year was obvious.

By comparing the will books, deed books, and tax records I came to the conclusion that Mildred Timbers was purchased from the Thomas Ingram estate. Estate sales were advertised in the local paper. I then read the *Richmond Enquirer* from December 1837 to Dec 1838. There were only two notices. The only one that appeared relevant is found below. Note that it really doesn't give any helpful information. Hopefully something else will be found and complete the search.

FAMILY NEGROES FOR SALE

For sale 15 or 20 likely young Negroes, including men, women, boys and girls. Among them is one first rate seamstress, and one woman a good house servant. The above Servants are as likely as can be found anywhere, and can be recommended to any gentleman who wishes to purchase for his own use. Such a lot is seldom in the market.

Inquire at the office of the Enquirer March 20   102.4t[1]

---

[1] *Richmond Enquirer*, Volume 34, Number 102, 20 March 1838, pg 2, Library of Virginia

INTRODUCTION

Will books are a good source in the search for slaves only if the owner named the slave(s). Many times a will lists property without specifying if it includes slaves. For example: "I will and bequeath to my (wife, son, daughter, etc.) all my estate both real and personal of every sort." or "...the property I have already given to my (wife, son, daughter, etc.)..." The documents often do not include the slave's name, sometimes only girl, runaway, boy, etc.

The documents in this manuscript include administrator's estate accounts, executor accounts, and inventories and appraisals. Will books 1742-1830 are located under Land and Property, the other will books are under Probate Records on the familysearch.org website.

Each slave owner is listed first followed by the page number, date and type of document. The list of slaves follows below. The new owner is listed if known. Surnames of the owner's children are indexed only if noted in the document.

Not included in this summary is a slave's monetary value, if the slave was sold, hired by the estate, hired out, or who hired the slave. The original text should be read to determine which occurred. Sometimes the estate or guardian account listed people paying money to the estate but not why the remittances were paid.

It is important to note the slave's age since the value of a slave increases or decreases with age and ability. It can also be used as a tracking tool. The ages are approximate.

When you read the digitized will books be aware that different spellings were used. Be creative in looking for first names: Seaser (Cesar), Ausker (Oscar), Fillis Phelice, Fillice, etc. Some names may be shortened, i.e. Cat could be Caty or Catherine.

Handwriting is sometimes difficult to read. In some cases I placed an underscore between letters (e.g. Mi_n_a). Names beginning with an underscore are indexed first (e.g. __mia). Some letters can be mistaken for others: "L" and "S", "T" and "F", J" and "I". The letter "n" can look like "u", "nn" could be "rr".

There are question marks next to some of the names and places where the handwriting is too faint or difficult to read. Be sure to peruse the entire index and the original document to make your own decision regarding the spelling of the name, county or town. You may discover a name that has a similar spelling to the one you are researching. Names can also appear more than once on a page.

Some of the pages are very faint. The quality of the films varies and some digitized copies were difficult to read. There were many guesses as to the written names and I take full responsibility for any errors in transcription.

The documents read for this volume are on microfilm held by the Family History Library at Salt Lake City. They are available on-line through Family History Centers.

I hope this book helps you to locate a slave or an owner. Good luck in your search.

ABBREVIATIONS

Admin - Administrator

Admin Acct – Administration account

Comm Acct – Committee Account

dec'd – deceased

Estate Acct – Estate Account

Exec Acct – Executor Account

Inv & Appr – Inventory & Appraisal

Gdn Acct – Guardian Account

Trustee Acct – Trustee Account

yrs - years

WILL BOOK VOL A
1835 – 1845

William HEADLEY, Frederick Co .... pg 1, 4 April 1835, Will

slaves to be divided into ten equal shares viz one share to the children of my deceased daughter Abigail SMITH, one share to my daughter Sarah LAN_ER, one share to the children of my deceased daughter Mary MILLER, one share to my son William HEADLY, one share to my daughter Winifred BROWNING, one share to the children of my deceased son James HEADLEY, one share to my daughter Elizabeth GUTHRIDGE, one share to my daughter Rebeca KENDRICK, one share in trust to my son Newton HEADLY for the use of my daughter Lucinda KENDRICK free and clear from her husband John KENDRICK and at her death to her children, one share to my son Newton HEADLY

Sarah HANSBROUGH, Frederick Co ....pg 2, 25 Aug 1834, Will

Hannah, Nancy, Janny, Elias, Abner, Ethelinda, Charity to daughter Margaret HANSBROUGH; Mariah, Mary, Sharlette, Rachel, Stephen, Annie, Abner, Jany? to daughter Lucy HANSBROUGH; Washington, Duff, Alcinda to son Presley HANSBROUGH

William HEADLEY .... pg 4, 17 May 1836, Inv & Appr

man Armstead, boy James, woman Peggy, girls Ann, Haner?, woman Rachel, girl Eliza, boys Moses? Mason?, Elias

....pg 6, 25 Aug 1836, Sales

Rachel & 6 children to Lucinda KENDRICK; Armested, Peggy & 6 children to William HEADLEY

Sarah ROLLINGS ....pg 11, 24 Feb 1837, Will

Edward, Henry, Adam given their freedom

Daniel SHAMBAUGH...................................... pg 12, 2_ Dec 1836, Will

Richard to daughter Mary to be free upon paying her the sum of $400 & John, born 26 Mar 1833, to serve her and be free when he is 25; woman Annah to daughter Margaret to be free upon paying her the sum of $300 & any children she may have prior to her payment to serve until they are 25, boy Jacob, born 27 May 1834, until he is 25 & then freed; boy Charles, born 29 Oct 1835, to daughter Rachel until he is 25 & then freed

Sarah HANSBROUGH .... pg 13, 20 Jan 1837, Inv & Appr

Hannah, Mariah, Jeny, Nancy, Charlotte & Henry, Alcinda, Mary, Elias, Ethelinda, George, Rachel, Abner, Ann, Duff, Nanny, Charity, Abner 2nd

Margaret HANSBROUGH .... pg 14, 10 Apr 1837, Inv & Appr

slaves named in a certain Bill filed in Circuit Court: women Hannah, Nancy, man Elias, girl Ethelinda, boy Abner, girls Nanny, Chasity

James BROWN .... pg 16, 15 Sept 1837, Inv & Appr

Henry?, Washington, Bailes Strawther, James, Jefferson, old Benjamin, Clara, Queen, Lucinda & child Richard, Daniel, Eliza, Caroline, Ann Sylvia, ___ & Mary, Margaret, Delia

Daniel SHAMBAUGH .... pg 17, 23 June 1837, Inv & Appr

The negroes are divided to certain of the legatees by Will: Richard (cart man), Hirena (Annah?) (female servant), John, Jacob?, Charles

Benjamin T. BUCKLEY .... pg 20, 27 Oct 1837, Inv & Appr

man Adam

William HEADLEY .... pg 23, 28 Apr 1836 - 23 Apr 1838, Estate Acct

negroes divided; negroes boarded; negroes at sale

Benjamin T. BUCKLEY .... pg 28, 27 Sept 1838, Sales

hire of old Betsy by R.M. TIMBERLAKE; hire of old Adam by James L. DAVIS; hire of boy ___ by T.W. THOMAS

James BOWEN, Fauquier Co .... pg 34, 18 Oct 1837, Sales

James & his wife to Joseph PAYNE

Martha RANDOLPH, Frederick Co .... pg 40, 16 Dec 1833, Will

Edmund, Rachel to grandson Thomas Beverly RANDOLPH & at his death Edmund to William May_ RANDOLPH & Rachel to Martha E. RANDOLPH with request that they leave them with their mother for hire, any female child of Rachel to great granddaughter Susan B.

RANDOLPH; Martha RANDOLPH is the daughter of James COCK? of Williamsburg

James BOWEN ....pg 43, 21 July 1837 – 3 Apr 1839, Estate Acct

Thornton hired; man Manuel sold; Lucy, Clara, Henry, Strother, Ann Sylvia, Mary, Manuel, Daniel, Alcinda, Sidney, Tom, girl, Louiza, Eveline, Elizabeth, Washington, Baalis, Jeffers, Ben, Queen

Samuel J. SHACKELFORD ....
....pg 48, 29 Mar 1837 – 30 Apr 1839, Estate Acct

Thornton; an old negro __mas died; Kate, Sanford; negroes divided; Hampson sold to John B. EARLE, ran off to Mrs? THOMAS

Robertson WAY ....pg 60, 8 July – 25 Sept 1839, Comm Acct

Edmond, a runaway slave in Pennsylvania; negroes sold; Edmond sold

Benjamin T. BUCKLEY ....
.... pg 66, 11 Nov 1837 – 16 Oct 1839, Estate Acct

Adam

Sarah RAWLINGS...pg 76, 5 May 1837, Sales

Edmund, a free man; Henry Strother, a free man – purchased goods

....pg 78, 29 May 1837 – 22 Oct 1839, Estate Acct

Edmund, Henry, Adam

Robertson WAY .... pg 80, 5 __ 1839, Inv & Appr

men Ralph, Frank, Tom, __, Iris & 3 children Lucy, Janny, & Eliza, Lydia & 4 children Nancy?, Elizabeth, Mary, & James?, girls Hannah, Louiza

Samuel GARDNER..pg 91, 5 July 1840, Will

woman Lucinda to wife Elizabeth; Sally, age 8, to niece Sarah Ann SWANN; James & Eliza Jr. to stepson Felix B. WELTON

Lewis PRIEST...............pg 99, 13 __ 1837? – 22 Sept? 1840, Estate Acct

Letty

John COMPTON .... pg 102, 30 May 1840, Will

> wife Dorcey to have choice of slaves, the remainder to be divided among the children - Peggy C. WHITE later Peggy C. COMPTON, William C. COMPTON, Laura? G. HADDON late Laura? G. COMPTON, Elizabeth E. RIDING?, late Elizabeth E. COMPTON, Elias E. COMPTON, John A. COMPTON, & Mary Ann C. HINKELY?, late Mary Ann C. COMPTON

Mary Ann CASE .... pg 103, 28 Nov 1840, Will

> girl Milly, boy Isaac to brother James CASE & after his death to his __; boy Jetson to brother Robert B. CASE & after his death to his son Albert; girl Rebecca to niece Margaret CASE daughter of James CASE; "...if my brother Elijah RICKETT will give me one servant boy little Reason that said Reason be given to my two brothers James and Robert B. CASE..."

Elijah ROY .... pg 104, 1 Aug 1836, Will

> man Lewis, woman Hannah, boy Jack, girl Marthina to son Gibson N. ROY; Sylvia, Hatty? & her 3 children to daughter Nancy GRANT; Amelia & her younger child Argus? to daughter Betsy MURPHY; Lucy, girl Matilda now in possession of Ab__ MURPHY & his wife Betsy to granddaughter Eldish daughter of Betsy MURPHY; girl Arthela to granddaughter Alcinda MURPHY daughter of Betsy MURPHY; girl Mirah to granddaughter, daughter of Polly LAWRENCE; girl Mariza to daughter Polly LAWRENCE; Edly to daughter Elizabeth MURPHY

Hannah CAIN .... pg 107, 24 Mar 1837 - 16 Apr 1839, Estate Acct

> Andrew FLEMMING kept & fed slaves belonging to the estate

Simon ALLENSWORTH .... pg 111, 8 May 1839, Inv & Appr

> man James

.... pg 112, 25 Jan 1841, Sales

> man to E. ALLENSWORTH

.... pg 116, Mar 1839 – 25 Jan 1841, Estate Acct

> Jim

4

John SELF .... pg 118, 8 Feb 1841, Sales

Frederick, Jim, Sukey, Mary, Jacob to John SELF, Alfred, Patty & child, Gordan, Sandy to Henry SELF, Sophy, Florinda to James COONRAD, Susannah, Fanny to Joseph COONRAD, Martha to John ROBISON, Eliza to James CROSS, Eveline to Judge WHITE, Ann Mariah to Isab/Isabelle? SHAMBAUGH

William HEADLY .... pg 120, 1838 – 1 Apr 1841, Estate Acct

legatees of slaves: Thomas & Sarah LAWLER, Elijah & Elizabeth GUTHRIDGE, the heirs of Abigail SMITH dec'd, Winifred BROWNING widow of Joseph BROWNING, Jacob & Rebecca KENDRICK, John W. MILLAR father & guardian of the children of Mary MILLAR dec'd, William HEADLY Jr., Mrs. Lucy KENDRICK, James D. HEADLY guardian of the heirs of James HEADLY dec'd

Daniel SHAMBAUGH...
.... pg 125, 11 Dec 1839 – 10 June 1841, Estate Acct

advancements and charges made against the heirs: Margaret SHAMBAUGH's negroes, Rachel SHAMBAUGH's negro Charles, Mary SHAMBAUGH's for negroes

William A. KING .... pg 127, 12 May 1841, Will

William, James to wife Maria Louisa KING & at her death to sister Mary KING & at her death to ___ Summerville KING

Catharine RICHARDSON ....
....pg 136, 22 Sept 1837 – 1 Feb 1839, Estate Acct

woman   Sylvia provided for by the Will of the late Samuel RICHARDSON

James BOWEN .... pg 140, 8 Aug 1839 – 5 July 1841, Estate Acct

Washington, Strother, Lucinda & children, Queen, Evelina, Sidney, Ben, Elizabeth, Jeff, Jim, Fanny, Lucy, Louisa, Morgan, Eliza, Margaret, & others retained by Mrs. BOWEN; Henry apprehended, jailed in Winchester, removed to Richmond; man Henry, Thornton; Baalis, Clary, Athalinda, Annsylvia, Mary kept by Mrs. BOWEN

William A. KING .... pg 144, 25 Aug 1841, Inv & Appr

man William; James age 9 belonging to the estate now in the possession of & claimed by Mrs. KING the mother of William A. KING

William HOPEWELL .... pg 145, 30 Sept 1837, Will

David, his wife Lucy, & the youngest child at present shall be free at my death & wish them to go to Liberia; George to be free at the age of 30, Matilda at the same time; Hamilton to be free at age 29, Henry at the same time; James to be free at age 30 & Sally at the same time; Aaron to be free at age 31 & Jefferson at the same time; all to go to Liberia including their children

John COMPTON .... pg 150, 15 Dec 1840, Inv & Appr

Stephen, Jerry, Ambrose, boys Joe, James, Moses, Tom, Anthony, Hamilton, Stephen, women Patty, Charlotte, Hannah, Judah, Caroline, Edna, Eliza, Sally, Kitty

Elijah ROY .... pg 157, 2 Jan 1841, Deposition of Servants

woman Hannah, boy Jack, girls Marthina, Mary, Lavina, _atena, boy Rex? in the possession of Gibson N. ROY; the 4 last mentioned were born since the date of the Will; woman Sylvia devised in the Will to Nancy GRANT but given in the lifetime of the dec'd to Mary Ann LOCHART together with her 2 youngest children O'Dalphin & Amanda; the husband of M.A. LOCHART has had them in his possession for 2 yrs & upwards; Kitty & her 3 children devised in the Will to Nancy GRANT in her possession for 5 yrs & upwards; Amelia & her youngest child Angus devised in the Will to Betsy MURPHY in her possession for 5 yrs & upwards; woman Melinda devised in the Will to granddaughter Lucy of daughter Betsy MURPHY in her possession for 5 yrs & upwards; woman Arthely devised in the Will to Alsinda MURPHY dec'd; woman Mariah devised in the Will to Susan LAWRENCE given by the dec'd since the date of his Will to Nancy GRANT in whose possession she has been more than 5 yrs; woman Mariga devised in the Will to Polly LAWRENCE given by the dec'd since the date of his Will to Jane LAWRENCE in her possession 2 yrs; Edly devised in the Will to Elizabeth MURPHY dec'd; boy Denis, girl Rachel children of Sylvia given by the dec'd since the date of his Will to Elizabeth LAWRENCE his granddaughter in her possession 1 yr

Benjamin F. BERKELY ....
...................................pg 160, 21 Apr 1840 – 4 Nov 1841, Estate Acct

man

William HOPEWELL ....pg 162, 5 Oct 1841, Inv & Appr

man David, Lucy & child, George, Matilda & 2 children Reuben & Harriet, Henrietta, Hamilton, James, Sarah, Aaron, Jefferson

Robertson WAY ....pg 166, 26 Sept 1839 - 1 Oct 1841, Estate Acct

Ralph, Iris & 3 children kept by William RANDOLPH, Frank, Tom, Willis, Louisa, Harriett, Lydia & 4 children

Mary Ann CASE ....pg 168, 30 Jan 1841, Inv & Appr

woman Milly, boys Isaac, Jetson, girl Rebecca

Thomas BUCK ....pg 170, 24 Oct 1839, Will

old negroes to be maintained by the estate; Harry, Jack to wife Ruhamah BUCK; old negreos to daughters Henretta CALMES & Letitia BLACKMORE or their heirs at the death of wife & daughter Miriam; Maria, Jane, Margaret, William to wife Ruhamah BUCK by Deed of Gift on 23 Apr 1834 including 2 children that Maria has had since that date

.... pg 172, 28 Oct 1839, Codicil

Ben to practice a trade; same to Jack after death of Ruhamah BUCK & he arrives at age 30; Sidney to wife

Thomas BLACKWOOD ....pg 172, 2 Aug 1838, Will

Isaac & Harry to daughters Massy BLACKWOOD & Polley BLACKWOOD as long as they are unmarried & then to sons James BLACKWOOD, Levi BLACKWOOD, Richard BLACKWOOD, Thomas BLACKWOOD, William BLACKWOOD, & daughters Rachel wife of Morgan ROWZEE, Sarah wife of Harrison WOOD

William HOPEWELL ....pg 174, 7 Oct 18__, Sales

boy James hired by Elias C. FINNELL, woman & 2 children, kept by John? HITE, boys Aaron, Jefferson to Neverson SMITH

Francis MARSHALL ....pg 176, 31 Jan 1840, Inv & Appr

man Alex

7

Francis MARSHALL .... pg 177, 31 Jan 1840, Sales

Alexander to William LEWIN

Samuel GARDNER......... pg 182, 29 Sept 1840 – 1 Oct 1842, Estate Acct

hire of negroes: Solomon to Robert TURNER then Mrs. E. GARDNER, Sam to Alexander FINNELL, Milly & children to Richard F. HALL then to Isaac HARRISON, Maria to John W. HALL then to Alexander FINNELL, Sally to William SHORES then to W.H. KENNER, Joe to M. OLIVER, George, Jim to James V. WEIR then George to Isaac HARRISON, Clarissa & children, Eliza to Mrs. E. GARDNER, Jack, Harriett & children to Joseph McCARTNEY, Lucinda & child to Robert LIPSCOMB

.... pg 188, 3 Oct 1840 – 1 Oct 1842, Estate Acct

Harriet, Jack; Joe hired from Samuel MYERS

William TAIT.. pg 191, 27 Aug 1842, Will

all negroes to wife Sarah TAIT; Elizabeth & her daughter Susan to daughter Martha TAIT; Caroline to daughter Mary TAIT; woman Frances Cuddelah?, girl Araminta for the support of old Lidda, who upon the death of my wife, can choose her mistress; girl Sary Ellend? to daughter Frances McCUBBIN

Sampson HOWELL ...... pg 194, 18 Dec 1837 – 14 Dec 1842, Estate Acct

negroes

Nancy McPHERSON .... pg 195, 31 July 1842, Will

Henry, William, Samuel, Sally, John, Minor to daughter & son-in-law Johnston & Mildred LAKE; Marian to grandson Harvey LAKE son of Johnston LAKE

William TAIT.. pg 205, 15 Dec 1842, Inv & Appr

Betsy, Lydia, Caroline, Nancy, Sall, Min_ Susan

William COOK .... pg 208, 1 Feb 1838, Will

wife Elizabeth to have choice of slaves & at her death to the children; maid & boy age 10 or 12 of her choice to daughter Lucy who was provided for by the Will of brother-in-law Samuel DAVENPORT, daughters Sarah, Mary wife of Winterton MURPHY, Nancy BEALE, & Marth MASON, & sons William, Giles, & Samuel

William COOK .... pg 211, 25 Jan 1841, 2nd Codicil

daughter Nancy's portion to go to her children Elizabeth C. BEALE, Giles C. BEALE, & Joseph C. BEALE when they are 21 yrs old; negroes may be sold if necessary

William R. ASHBY.. pg 212, 25 Jan 1841, Will

wife Rebecca R. ASHBY; negroes may be sold if necessary, to stay in Virginia, families to be kept together

Thomas BLACKWOOD .... pg 214, 17 Aug 1842, Inv & Appr

Isaac, Harry

Chancy GATEWOOD........................... pg 215, 24 Aug 1842, Inv & Appr

men Robert, Elias, Abraham, boy Martin, woman Patsy, girls Mary Susan, Martha, Mary & child

James BOWEN .... pg 224, 2 Dec 1841 – 23 June 1843, Estate Acct

Lucy, Evelina & child, Alcinda, Wash, Strother, Ben, Jim, Jeff, Sidney, Fanny, Elizabeth, Louisa, Margaret, Queen, Lucinda & children, Eliza, Baalis, Clary, Annsylvia, Mary

William A. KING ....pg 226, June 1841 – 16 Aug 1843, Estate Acct

servant; boy willed to M.L HALL, late M.L. KING & her present husband Richard T. HALL

Lewis LAWRENCE .... pg 228, 18 Aug 1842 – 1 July 1843, Estate Acct

John Stinson in jail (relationship not known)

William HOPEWELL .... pg 234, 7 Oct 1841 – 1 Oct 1843, Estate Acct

Lucy, Hamilton, David, James, George, Aaron, Jefferson, Matalda & 2 children, Henretta, Sarah, Sally

.... pg 236, 22 Oct 1842 – 1 Oct 1843, Estate Acct

hire of negroes: George to R.E. FINNELL, Hamilton to Russell FINNELL, James to A.? FINNELL then Thomas LAKE, Aaron to R.S. LONG then E. ANDREWS, Jefferson to N.SMITH then to J. McKAY, Matilda & 2 children to John HITE, Henrietta to J. TROUT, Sarah to J._. PETTY then John SELF

Robertson WAY ....pg 242, 25 Dec 1841 – 1 Oct 1843, Estate Acct

Lydia & children kept by James WAY, Iris & children kept by Neverson SMITH, daughter of Lydia died in April last, woman & girl

negro hires: Frank, Tom, Lydia & children to James WAY, Ralph to Nancy WAY then to William HEADLY, Willis to James N. WEIR then to James WAY, Louisa, Harriet to C. KENDRICK, Iris & children to William RANDOLPH then to Neverson SMITH, Louisa to T.W. THOMAS

Isaac OVERALL ....pg 246, 19 May 1843, Inv & Appr

men Charles, Bill

....pg 248, 23-24 June 1843, Sales

men Charles, Bill to G.N. ROZE

William RILEY ....pg 252, 20 Dec 1843 – 27 Dec 1842, Estate Acct

negro

William MONROE ....pg 256, 18 July 1836, Will

Alexander, Reuben, Jeffrey, Will, Frances, China & her children to wife Ann MONROE & at her death Will & Frances to choose their owners; slaves to sons William MONROE, Thomas MONROE, George MONROE, & John MONROE, daughters Catharine NEUMAN, Sarah NEUMAN, Mary LEACH, & Eliza MONROE; China & her children to daughter Sarah NEUMAN, Alexander to daughter Mary LEACH, Jeffrey to son John MONROE, & Reuben to daughter Eliza MONROE at the death of their mother Ann MONROE

.... pg 257, 20 July 1842, Codicil

bequeaths to son John MONROE revoked & given to James R. RICHARDS ___ for Ethelinda MONROE, wife of son John MONROE, & her children; Jeffrey to daughter Eliza MONROE instead of Reuben

Samuel GARDNER...pg 257, 27 Dec 1843, Sales

George, girls Emma, Maria, & Mary, Harriet & 2 children, old man Sam, boy Charles to Samuel B. GARDNER, Milley & child, boys William, Harrison, Jack, & Joe, Clarissa & 1 child to Robert M. ALLEN, old man Solomon to R. KNISALY? for T.L. BLACKMAN, girl Betty to Richard H. TIMBERLAKE

Samuel J. SHACKELFORD ....
.... pg 260, 1 July 1842 – 1 July 1844, Estate Acct

negro

Capt. Thomas BUCK, Front Royal ....pg 266, 6 Oct 1843, Inv & Appr

Ben 56, woman Sidney 23, Alexander 6, Martha 3, Charles 7 months

Joshua ANTRAM...pg 266, 7 Sept 1844, Will

½ of the slaves to wife Pamelia, also the present infant child of Janella; one negro of her own choosing to Elizabeth McKAY; girl to Nancy McKAY wife of Robert McKAY; girl to Sarah BUCK wife of Charles BUCK; girl to Eliza BUCK wife of John BUCK, "…the four hereby bequeathed bring all that I own with the exception of the infant given to my wife as above."

Thomas BUCK............. pg 268, 12 Aug 1842 - 19 Sept 1844, Estate Acct

Ben; Harry died?

Samuel GARDNER...........pg 270, 3 Nov 1842 - 8 Aug 1844, Estate Acct

Lucinda & child, Milly & children, girl Eliza; negro sold; old Solomon, Sam, George, Joe, Sally, Nelly & child, Clarissa & child, Jackson, Maria, Harriet & children; girl Betty purchased by Richard H. TIMBERLAKE on 27 Dec 1843

Martha TRIPLETT .... pg 274, 8 Apr 1844, Inv & Appr

man Lewis, woman Ann

Samuel BUCK... pg 275, 12 Dec 1844, Will

old woman Milly to nephew John G. BUCK; Liddy, Emmaly, Judy servants of brother John BUCK

Francis MARSHALL ....pg 276, 27 Mar 1840 – 16 Dec 1844, Estate Acct

man Alexander sold; the widow gets 1/3 of the slaves, the rest to be divided into 8 shares

Joshua ANTRAM................................. pg 286, 21 Apr 184_, Inv & Appr

man Philip, woman Evelina, Genitta? & child, girls Amanda, Julia

11

John COMPTON ....pg 294, 31 Oct 1842 – 3 May 1845, Estate Acct

deficiency in amount of her, Dorea COMPTON, dower in slaves

Margaret RICKETTS ....pg 296, 5 Oct 1843, Dower Negroes

"...to divide the dower negroes of Margaret RICKETTS dec'd among those entitled thereto...heirs of Anna Case REASON Jr & Jerry, ...Elijah RICKETTS & Gerard C. Ricketts REASON Sr.; Margaret, Sidney, & Jilson..."

William A. KING ....pg 307, 16 Aug 1843 – 1 Sept 1845, Estate Acct

boy Jim bought on 20 Aug 1837 from Virlinda KING admix of August KING dec'd

William COOK .... pg 310, 14 Dept 1843 – 1 Oct 1845, Estate Acct

Bob apprehended, in jail; Bob, boy George sold; woman Charlotte, Shadrack, Thornton, girls Peggy, Louisa, woman Aley, boy _anison, woman Sally, boy Solomon

John McKAY ....pg 313, 9 Jan 1846, Inv & Appr

girl Frances, Malinda & 2 children, Levina, Caroline & child

Robertson WAY ....pg 314, 25 Dec 1843 – 1 Oct 1845, Estate Acct

Iris & children kept by Thomas B. RANDOLPH, Lydia & children kept by Neverson SMITH, girl Nancy, Louisa at C. KENDRICKS, Lydia at Thomas BROWN's, Harriett at Mrs. THOMAS; Frank, Tom, Ralph, Willis, girl, Lucy

William TIMBERLAKE ....pg 316, 8 Mar 1844, Will

choice of servant each to daughters Mary Ann & Harriett; boy George to daughter Elizabeth in place of the boy given to her that died; remaining servants to be divided among all children: John, Mary Ann, Frances, Alice, William, Elizabeth & Harriett and son R.M.S. TIMBERLAKE's widow; servant Peter to R.M.S. TIMBERLAKE's widow?

William HOPEWELL .... pg 323, 1 Jan 1844 – 1 Jan 1846, Estate Acct

negroes kept at John HITE & at David F_AKS, Matilda & 2 children kept at A. MENIFER

Susannah RILEY .... pg 328, 25 Sept 1845, Sales

"This inventory of sales of personal Estate of George RILEY dec'd on hand at the death of his widow Susannah RILEY who had a life estate therein was returned and ordered to be recorded."

old Sam to Charles B. RUST

Henry SELF .... pg 331, 11 Nov 1844, Will

boy Duskin to be freed & sent to Ohio; Jordan 13, & Sandy 11 to be put to the blacksmith trade for a term of 7 years & then set free & sent to Ohio; Sydnor 18 & Alfred 27 to be hired for a term of 7 years and then freed; ..."Patty 50 to have her choice to be manumitted & set free together with her daughter Rachel & go the the state of Ohio with Duskin or to remain with my brother John SELF for the term of 7 years and be freed & go to Ohio..."

Alfred D. ASHBY .... pg 333, 15 Oct 1845, Inv & Appr

Peggy & child, James, Mary, Baalis, John, Sarah

.... pg 335, 16 Oct 1845, Sales

Peggy & child to Charles B. RUST; Jim, John to A.R. FUNSTEN; Mary to B. ASHBY; Baalis to John B. EARLE; Sarah to William _. SMITH

James BOWEN .... pg 340, 28 Dec 1843 – 1 Apr 1846, Estate Acct

Elizabeth, Evelina & child, Lucinda & child, Lucy, Alcinda, Margaret, Eliza kept by Walter BOWEN, Sidney, Fanny, Ben, Wash, Jeff, Louisa & child, Queen; other negroes returned by Mrs. BOWEN; Richard

.... pg 342, Appended Estate Acct

Baalis, Clara, Strother, Jim, Mary, Annsylvia

Peter CATLETT .... pg 346, 29 Sept 1843 – 1 Mar 1846, Estate Acct

girl Nancy to Eli ANDERSON

Martha TRIPLETT .... pg 347, 15 July 1844 – 1 Jan 1846, Estate Acct

girl Mary, Lewis, Ann

Selby FOLEY .... pg 359, 13 Jan 1843, Will

Eli, Hannah to choose their masters after the death of wife Rachel FOLEY

Thomas BUCK .... pg 362, 19 Sept 1844 – 1 Sept 1846, Estate Acct

Ben, old Judy

Rhody SMITH .... pg 366, 30 Sept 1838, Will

Hannah & all her children to be freed; boy Isaac with brother Elisha SMITH in Ohio to be freed when he arrives at the age of 21 on 2 June 1843

.... pg 366, 6 Oct 1846, Codicil

"confirm…Hannah & her children…as well the small children now at home as Lewis & James who are hereby emancipated after serving Abed CRABILL until they shall respectively arrive at the age of 21…"

Samuel GARDNER ...... pg 367, 13 Nov 1844 – 13 Nov 1846, Estate Acct

Lucinda; purchase of slaves; Harriett & child kept by Thornton LEACH; Maria, Joe

Selby FOLEY .... pg 374, 16 Mar 1846 – 26 Jan 1847, Comm Report

Eli

William MONROE .... pg 378, 31 Aug 1845 - 23 Dec 1846, Estate Acct

Alex, Jeffrey; Alex & Jeffrey sold

William TIMBERLAKE .... pg 382, 7 Mar 1846, Inv & Appr

Hannah & child Peter, Elijah, Emanuel, James, Lewis & Louisa his wife, Sarah, Amelia, Alfred

Selby FOLEY .... pg 383, 26 Feb 1847, Inv & Appr

woman Hannah, man Eli

Alexander MURPHY .... pg 386, 17 Feb 1846, Will

man Angus, woman Euphemia & child Ben to wife Elizabeth MURPHY & at her death to son John Lewis MURPHY; girl Alice to daughter Alcinda Ann LAWRENCE wife of James M. LAWRENCE;

woman Mahala to son Grafton MURPHY, woman Milley, girl Regina to son John Lewis MURPHY

Marcus C. BUCK .... pg 388, 13 July 1845 - 1 June 1846, Estate Acct

Dick; Joe advertised; Ann & increase

Alexander MURPHY .... pg 395, 15 June 1847, Inv & Appr

girl, servant & 3 children, servant, boy, girl

Reuben E. FINNELL .... pg 396, 26 Aug 1843 - 9 Oct 1847, Estate Acct

negro

Alfred D. ASHBY .... pg 400, 1 Oct 1845 - 6 Sept 1847, Estate Acct

slaves sold

Rhoda SMITH .... pg 407, 24 Oct 1846, Inv & Appr

woman Hannah, boys Lewis, James, Joseph, girl Mary, boy Daniel

Jason THOMPSON .... pg 408, 3 Sept 1847, Dower Slaves

Matilda, boy Buck to widow Lucretia THOMPSON; boy Bud Eason, girl Mary Harlow, General Henry Lee, girl Flora, boy Polk ___, boy Gilbert Bebee

Mary Harlow to Edmund THOMPSON; Bud Eason to Isaiah WOOD & wife; Polk ___ to Benjamin THOMPSON; General Henry Lee to Jesse THOMPSON; Flora to James PRATT & wife; Gilbert B Bee to John E. THOMPSON

William FRISTOE, Jr. .... pg 408, 15 Sept 1846, Dower Slaves

Ginny, Harret, Silvia to widow Lucy FRISTOE, her third; John, Mary to Silas, Susan, Elizabeth, Sarah, Priscilla, & Lucy FRISTOE; Ann & 2 of her children, Clary & Elias, to Nancy, Mariam, Julia, & Jane the 4 other heirs

Christopher KENDRICK .... pg 410, 15 Dec 1847, Will

slaves may be sold if necessary for debts, the residue to wife & at her death to 5 children

William COOK .... pg 412, 1 Oct 1845 – 1 Jan 1848, Estate Acct

man Shadrack sold; hire of Alsey to Giles COOK, Sally to Ewell BAKER, Shadrack to J. CROSS, Lotty, Solomon to James CARPER

15

then Solomon to J.S. BURNS, Peggy to A.M. CLINE, Louisa to P. JOHNSTON, Phebe to M. CLOUD, Granison to W. BOWEN, Ben to W. CLARK then to John P__ER, Nancy to Alexander CATLETT, Philip to M. PIERCE then to John PERRY; man Alec sold

John SELF .... pg 423, 25 Jan 1848, Inv & Appr

Frederick, Samuel, Aaron, Jacob, Mary & 3 children

.... pg 425, 27 Jan 1848, Sales

slaves hired: Samuel to William R. JOHNSON; Aaron to Samuel M. S__GLER; Jacob to Thomas _. RANDOLPH; Mary & 3 children kept by William CONRAD who hired Frederick

William TIMBERLAKE .... pg 432, 9 Mar 1846, Sales

Lewy & wife, Elijah to R.H. TIMBERLAKE; Alfred, Manuel to J.? TIMBERLAKE; Cornelia, Peter to Mrs. M.A. TIMBERLAKE

.... pg 434, 31 Mar 1846 - 9 June 1847, Estate Acct

bill of personal property included slaves

Christopher KENDRICK .... pg 438, 7 Feb 1848, Inv & Appr

woman, Alech, Daniel, girl Ann, boy Edmund, Frank, girl Harriet, men Jim, Bill, Grayson, boy Bob, Mildred & child Ben, girl Jane, boy Broaddus, Patty & child, girl Emily

.... pg 440, 11 Feb 1848, Inv & Appr

Jim, men Robbin, Tom, Frank, woman Mary, girls Elizabeth, woman Jane

Martha TRIPLETT .... pg 442, 1 Jan 1846 – 1 Jan 1848, Estate Acct

woman Ann died in Apr 1846; Lewis

Thomas BUCK .... pg 444, 1 Sept 1846 - 1 Sept 1848, Estate Acct

Judy, Ben

Rhoda SMITH .... pg 448, 24 Oct 1846 – 15 Nov 1848, Estate Acct

Hannah; slaves emancipated in accordance with Rhoda SMITH's Will

Margaret HAYNIE .... pg 450, 24 Dec 1848, Inv & Appr

Caroline & child Lucy

Charles CHURCHILL ....pg 450, 20 Sept 18_5, Will

Bill, Eliza, Henry, man Lewis Charles Churchill to daughter Sarah & at her death divided among all my children: Charles, John, Martha, Nancy, Elizabeth, Mariah, & Julia Ann; boy Henry, girl Winney to daughter Margaret; Howard, Lydia to daughter Lucinda; boy Tillenan to daughter Nancy, now in her possession; boy Arch to daughter Mariah, now in her possession; girl Fanny to daughter Martha, now in her possession; Henny Ash & her child Mary to Charles & John CHURCHILL in trust for daughter Julia Ann, wife of Richard BROWN; girl Betty to Charles & John CHURCHILL in trust for daughter Elizabeth, wife of Alexander SIMPSON; woman Delilah, boy Sam to daughter Susan; Bill age 6, boy George to son Charles; man Marlbrough to son John; remaining slaves to be divided among the children mentioned above

John M. ELLIOTT` .... pg 453, 24 Nov 1847, Inv & Appr

woman & 2 children, Lindsey & Winney, girls May Agnes, Haidenia, men Jim, Little George, Benjamin, old Big George, woman Polly, girl Caroline, Malinda & 2 children Nelson & Richard, girls Chartel, Sarah, Mary Elizabeth

....pg 456, 2_ Nov 1867, Sales

man George to John W. MEADE; girl Caroline to James W. MASON; man George to John STEWART; woman & children to James. W. WALKER; man Jim, boy Ben to Thornton P. PENDLETON

John SELF ....pg 462, 19 Mar 1849, Inv & Appr

Frederick, Samuel, Aaron, Jacob, Mary & 3 children

Selby FOLEY .... pg 466, 11 Jan 1847 – 1 Apr 1849, Estate Acct

Ely, Hannah

Thomas JOHN ....pg 469, 27 Apr 1849, Will

"...Charlotte shall be free immediately after my death on condidition that she shall never hereafter live with, or have any intercourse with Charles Posey, who has been her husband for a number of years, but if she shall violate this condition, it is my will that she shall remain a slave."; Mary Ann 23 shall be free 3 years after my death & she can chose her home; George, Richard, Catharine, Louisa, Martha to be free 15 years after my death & may be hired out or sold

Mary AMISS, Culpeper Co..............................pg 470, 25 Sept 1845, Will

woman Dolly to daughter Catharine STEEL; boy William Henry to daughter Mary Ann AMISS

....pg 474, 23 June 1849, Inv & Appr

William age 16

Charles CHURCHILL.............................pg 478, 8 Mar 1849, Inv & Appr

men Page, Bill, Lewis, Sam, George, Sidney & her child Russell, women Mary, Eliz, boy Henry, Jordan, Louisa, Winney, Ambrose, Delilah, Catharine, Charles, girls Mary, Eliza, Henny & her child Susan, boys Milton, Moses, Albert

WILL BOOK VOL B
1849 – 1856

John M. ELLIOTT .... pg 8, 24 Nov 1847 – 1 Nov 1848, Estate Acct

 amount of sales of slaves

Martha TRIPLETT .... pg 12, Mar - Dec 1849, Estate Acct

 Lewis sold

Christopher KENDRICK ....pg 14, 19 Aug 1848, Sales

 (pg 21) negroes hired: Emily to John R. JACKSON, Robin, Jim, Elizabeth, Mildred & child to William S. KENDRICK, Frank to John B. RUST, Edmund to George T. MASSIE, Frank to Abdel DAVIS, Mary to John MILLER

 .... pg 22, 14 Jan – 24 Dec 1849, Estate Acct

 slaves hired same as above

James R. ASH .... pg 30, Aug 1847 – 20 Aug 1849, Gdn Acct

 Iris & children kept by James CROSS, Lydia & children kept by John GLASSCOCK; Louisa ran away, apprehended, jailed

 slave hire: Ralph, Louiza & Jim, Jane, Eliza, Nancy, Lucy, Frank; paid Mrs. Nancy ULAY in division of slaves, Iris died

James SHUMATE .... pg 35, 17 Dec 1849, Inv & Appr

 woman Easter, girls Adaline, Hanner, Suesa? Luesa?, Alsay, boy David

Nancy TIMBERLAKE .... pg 39, 8 June 1846, Will

 George, John, Willison, Letty emancipated; old Winney to Walter BOWEN

Jonathan B. LEHEW .... pg 40, 1 Nov 1848 - 5 Jan 1850, Gdn Acct

 Sarah & child, Maria & child; dower slaves allotted to widow Ann LEHEW, the residue of the slaves have been allotted out to the heirs & hired out; Newton

19

Elizabeth LEHEW .... pg 42, 14 July 1847 - 5 Jan 1850, Gdn Acct

Sarah & child, Maria & child; dower slaves allotted to widow Ann LEHEW, the residue of the slaves have been allotted out to the heirs & hired out; Newton

Charles Edwin LEHEW .... pg 44, 1 Nov 1848 - 5 Jan 1850, Gdn Acct

Sarah & child, Maria & child; dower slaves allotted to widow Ann LEHEW, the residue of the slaves have been allotted out to the heirs & hired out; Newton

Francis Wesly LEHEW .... pg 46, 1 Nov 1848 - 5 Jan 1850, Gdn Acct

Sarah & child, Maria & child; dower slaves allotted to widow Ann LEHEW, the residue of the slaves have been allotted out to the heirs & hired out; Newton

Samuel REEL .... pg 49, 26 Dec 1849, Inv & Appr Slaves

men Eli, Edmund, boys Landon, William, Albert

.... pg 50, 27 Dec 1849, Sales

Eli to Joseph TROUT, private sale; public sales: Edmund to Joseph KENNER; William to O.R. FUNSTEN; Landon, Albert to C.H. GREEN

John SELF .... pg 56, 1 Jan 1848 - 15 Jan 1850, Estate Acct

Aaron ran away, apprehended, jailed; Mary & children kept by William S. CONRAD; Aaron sold

William B. HAND .... pg 60, 18 Feb 1850, Inv & Appr

"William B. HAND's re__sion__ of interest in Hester and her seven children & Washington"

Jason THOMPSON .... pg 61, 2 Sept 1847, Inv & Appr

Matilda 43, Buck 14, Bud Eastham 11, Mary Harlow 9, General Lee 7, Flora 5, boy Pold (Polk) _ Dallas 4, Gilbert B Bee 2

Thomas JOHN .... pg 69, 1 June 1849, Inv & Appr

Richard, George, Catharine, Louisa, Mary Ann, Martha, Charlotte/Sharlotte

20

Thomas JOHN .... pg 70, 2 June 1849, Sales

Richard to William BEATY; Catharine to George W. SKELTON; Louisa to John CANON; Charlotte to Thomas WILSON

Marcus C. BUCK .... pg 82, 1 June 1847 – 1 June 1849, Estate Acct

man Joe sold to Joel W. JONES; old woman Betty died

Jonathan B., Elizabeth, Charles Edwin, & Francis Wesley LEHEW .... pg 89, 24 Jan – 24 May 1850, Gdn Acct

man Newton, Sarah & child, Maria & child

John M. ELLIOTT .... pg 105, 26 Nov 1847, Inv & Appr

Melinda & 3 children Henry, Richard, & George sold to Richard BAYARLY on 8 Sept 1849; girls Mary, Sarah, Charlotte sold same time; woman Billy sold to Isaac HARRISON 11 July 1850

Daniel FUNKHOUSER, Shenandoah Co .... pg 107, 29 Mar 1839, Will

slaves to be divided among grandchildren William D. FUNKHOUSER & Mary FUNKHOUSER children of Jacob FUNKHOUSER dec'd, & daughter Eliza BAKER wife of Samuel BAKER, son Issac FUNKHOUSER, sons-in-law Daniel SHAMBOUGH considered as a part of his wife's share & Philip BORDEN considered as a part of his wife's share

George B. ASH .... pg 112, 25 Nov 1850, Inv & Appr

Harriet & G children, Samuel

Thomas BUCK .... pg 114, 1 Sept 1848 - 1 Sept 1851, Estate Acct

Ben; Judy died

Presley HANSBROUGH .... pg 118, 18 July 1848, Will

Lydia & her 3 children James, Mary, & Thornton, Ethelinda & her 2 children John & Anthony, Gustavus, Thomas to wife Mary W. HANSBROUGH & at her death to be sold

Lucy HANSBROUGH .... pg 119, 24 Mar 1851, Will

Jeny?, Fielding, Peter to nephew John HANSBROUGH & at his death to his children; "...all my slaves not herein before disposed of be emancipated and set free after the expiration of four years after my death namely Charlotte, Ethelinda, Louisa, Mariah, Catharine, Ann, Mary, Rachael, Henry…their removal to Liberia"

John RUST .... pg 121, 30 Jan 1851, Will

man Dan, woman Dilly, one of my youngest negroes of her choice to wife Elizabeth & sold at her death but man Dan & woman Dilly to chose which family they will serve; grandson John W.F. BROADUS to surrender a boy & woman to be regarded as part of the estate

Nancy TIMBERLAKE...
.... pg 124, 15 Feb 185_ - 12 Feb 1857, Estate Acct

legacies to Letty, John, George, William

Mandly TAYLOR ....pg 126, 20 Apr 1851, Will

Allick, Susan, Henry to granddaughter Ann Mariah BOWEN; girl Caroline to granddaughter Margaret WHEELRIGHT; small girl Mary, one of Eliz's children, to granddaughter Susan BUCK; Parlor & Mary his wife their freedom; the residue of the slaves to grandchildren Marcus BUCK, Mary Catharine WHEATLY, Mary BUCK, Catharine BUCK, Ann WHEATLY, Susan BUCK, Mandly WHEATLY, James WHEATLY, & George WHEATLY; old woman Fanny, man Tom

John McDANIEL .... pg 127, 7 May 1851, Inv & Appr

Ann & child Elias, Susan, Calvin, John, Seven, Mariah, Jeremiah, Ann Virginia

Richard RIDGEWAY...pg 133, 2 Sept 1851, Will

slaves to be freed after death of wife

Jonathan B. LEHEW .... pg 134, 7 Mar 1850 – 14 July 1851, Gdn Acct

Maria & child, Newton, Sarah & child

Ann Elizabeth LEHEW ..... pg 136, 7 Mar 1850 – 14 July 1851, Gdn Acct

Maria & child, Newton, Sarah & child

Edwin LEHEW .... pg 138, 7 Mar 1850 – 14 July 1851, Gdn Acct

Maria & child, Newton, Sarah & child

Francis Wesley LEHEW ... pg 140, 7 Mar 1850 – 14 July 1851, Gdn Acct

Maria & child, Newton, Sarah & child

Mandly TAYLOR .... pg 142, 20 May 1851, Inv & Appr

Moses 41, John 15, Washington 13, Frank 15, Ambrose 11, little Parlor 10, Eliza, Parlor 48 (set free), Mary 40 (set free), Bob 19, Alfred 28, Eliza 34 & infant Alfred, Mary Ann 40 & Josiah 4, Amelia 31 & children Betty 4 & George 2, Jacob 13, Ben 10, Joshua 14, Tasco 19, Margaret 20, Grend__ 29, Charles 41, Catharine 14, Ann Maria 12, Allick 7, Jim 13, William 4, Edmund 7, Mary 5, Tom 40, old Fanny 66, Thomison 14

Selby FOLEY .... pg 145, 1 Apr 1849 - 1 Apr 1851, Estate Acct

Hannah & child, Eli, Jeremiah

John M. ELLIOTT .... pg 148, 3 Feb 1849 - 1 July 1851, Estate Acct

Malinda & her 3 children Henry, Richard, & George sold to Richard BRYARLY; girls Mary, Charlotte sold to John MURRELL; girl Sarah sold to John JOLLIFFE, all sold at public auction at White Post; old woman Polly sold to Isaac HARRISON

Richard RIDGEWAY .... pg 152, 21 Sept 1851, Inv & Appr

Mariah, Margarett, Charles, Adam, Mariah Jr, Mary, Harriet, Jesse, Martin, Fanny Ann, William, Meredith, infant Sarah

Samuel REEL .... pg 154, 21 Mar 1849 - 21 July 1851, Estate Acct

man Edmund; boy Albert sold; lot of slaves sold; boy William, Eli, boy Landon

Ruhamah M. BUCK .... pg 169, 3 Apr 1846, Will

Maria Cooper & her children Jane, Margaret, William, Roxy, John, & Ruhamah, to be emancipated; man Philip Askins to be emancipated after a year passes; boys William Henry, Charles to be hired out until age 21 & then emancipated after a year passes

.... pg 171, 16 Aug 1851, 3rd Codicil

"...the children of my female servants born since the date of my Will & which may hereafter be born shall also be free..."

James R. ASH .... pg 174, 15 Sept 1849 – 28 Dec 1850, Gdn Acct

negro children kept by B.P. SILLMAN; Nancy, Louisa, Lydia & her children, Eliza, Ralph, Tom, Jane, Jim

Mandly TAYLOR ....pg 180, 13 Aug 1851, Sales

slaves hired out: Alfred, Bob, John, Washington, James, Moses, wife & children & 2 other children to George T. WHEATLY; Frank to W. BOWEN; Ambrose, Parlour Jr. to James CROSS; Eliza to John B. TAYLOR; Eliza, Alfred, Edmund, Amelia, Betty, George to George T. WHEATLY

Christopher KENDRICK ....
....pg 192, 16 Jan 1850 – 19 Mar 1851, Estate Acct

boy; Mary & child died in March; Frank, Robin, Jim, Edmond, Mildred & children, Elizabeth, Emily, Newman; hire of Frank from W.A. CARTER to 25 Aug when he ran away & was sold by Mrs. KENDRICK the widow; hire of Edmond to 31 May from James MANCH? when he ran away & was sold by Mrs. KENDRICK the widow

Thomas JOHN................pg 196, 25 July 1849 - 7 Sept 1851, Estate Acct

old Charlotte, George Posey, Richard, Catharine, Louisa, Martha, Mary Ann; George Posey sold having run away from John LEACH, apprehended & jailed

Jacob McKAY..pg 204, 13 Apr 1848, Will

"...my blacks save one...among children Nancy A. McKAY wife of R.S. McKAY, Jesse H. McKAY, Sarah J. BUCK wife of Charles BUCK, Eliza BUCK wife of John G. BUCK, & William B. McKAY..."

....pg 205, 7 June 1852, Codicil

Ben to son Thomas B. McKAY, Henry to son Oscar McKAY after the death of my wife Elizabeth

Nancy TIMBERLAKE.....pg 206, 7 Mar 1851 - 12 Feb 1842, Estate Acct

servant

Margaret CHURCHILL ....pg 213, 17 Oct 1849, Will

girl Winney to sister Susan CHURCHILL & brother John CHURCHILL; boy Henry to brother John CHURCHILL

John McDONALD ....pg 217, 8 Oct 1852, Inv & Appr

Ann & daughter Jane, boy Calvin, Susan & child Dilly, girl Maria, boys Stephen, John

Ann Elizabeth LEHEW .... pg 228, 6 Aug 1851 – 1 Jan 1853, Gdn Acct

Newton, Maria & child, Sarah & child

Charles Edwin LEHEW .... pg 230, 6 Aug 1851 – 1 Oct 1852, Gdn Acct

Newton, Maria & child, Sarah & child

Francis Wesley LEHEW ...... pg 232, 6 Aug 1851 – 1 Oct 1852, Gdn Acct

Newton, Maria & child, Sarah & child

Mandly TAYLOR .... pg 234, 20 May 1851 -15 Oct 1852, Estate Acct

old negroes supported by G.T. WHEATLEY

Presley HANSBROUGH .... pg 236, 2 Apr 1851, Inv & Appr

woman Lydia, girl Mary, boys Martin, Gustavus, Tom, John, Thornton, Anthony, Presley, woman Ethelinda, girl Edwina, boy James

.... pg 237, 13 Apr 1851, Sales

boy Tom to Thomas HUNT; boy Gustavus to R.B. BRASHEAR?

William HOPEWELL .... pg 248, 1847 - 1 Jan 1853, Estate Acct

Matilda & children kept by A. MENIFER; Hamilton, Sally, Aaron, Jim

Rebecca GARDNER .... pg 252, 22 Dec 1852, Will

Mary 15 & Frances 11, daughters of Harriet, to son Robert M. ALLEN; Harriet 30 & 2 children Ann Maria 7 & Betsy 4 months; Newton 14, son of Kitty & recently purchased from Robert M. ALLEN & S.B. GARDNER, to daughter Sarah C. GARDNER wife of Samuel B. GARDNER; Charles 13 & Charlotte 2, children of Harriet, to son Jonathan B. GARDNER

Elizabeth RUST.................................... pg 253, 15 Aug 1851, Inv & Appr

Daniel, Del, Ann are slaves devised to Elizabeth RUST, widow of John Rust dec'd, by his last Will

Reuben A. FINNELL ......pg 284, 7 Jan 1852 - 19 Dec 1853, Trustee Acct

trust fund to benefit Mordicai CLOUD, Vianne FINNELL, H. FINNELL & others; trust deed to Jacob for slaves

James R. ASH .... pg 288, 20 Aug 1851 - 6 Dec 1852, Gdn Acct

Jane, Ralph, Eliza, Nancy, Lucy

Franklin W. MASSIE .... pg 290, 6 Dec 1852, Inv & Appr

Turner, Daniel, Harriet

Robert M. ALLEN .... pg 295, 11 Oct 1853, Will

State of Missouri, County of Boone, in County Court, 20 Dec 1853

Polly & her 2 children Bill & Martha to wife Mary E. ALLEN; remainder of slaves to be divided between brother John B. GARDNER & sister Sarah C. GARDNER

Vincent SETTLE.. pg 298, 5 Dec 1853, Will

girl Ann to wife Catharine SETTLE; upon death or marriage slaves to be divided between children execpt Ann is to go to daughter Henrietta T. SETTLE

John McDONALD .... pg 312, Mar - Oct 1851, Estate Acct

boy Jerry sold, burying? boy, woman

James R. ASH .... pg 318, 28 Dec 1852 – 1 Jan 1854, Gdn Acct

Lydia & 6 children kept by T.V. HICKS; Eliza, Ralph, Nancy, Richard

Giles COOK, Trustee for certain creditors..
.... pg 320, Dec 1851 - Feb 1853, Receipts

girl Sarah to A.G. CHENSMITH; boy George to William B. BROWNER

John R. JACKSON, Trustee for certain creditors.......................................
.... pg 330, 6 Mar 1852 – 11 May 1853, Receipts

boy to Samuel C. RICHARDSON

Vincent SETTLE.................................... pg 332, 1 Apr 1854, Inv & Appr

men John, Sandy, boys Simon, Moses, girls Mary, Ann, women Eliza, Jane

27

Jacob McKAY...pg 338, 31 July 1854, Inv & Appr

old woman Nannie, girl Mary, man John, woman Eliza, girls Manda, Milly

Franklin H. MASSIE.......pg 346, 8 Nov 1852 – 16 Feb 1854, Estate Acct

Daniel, Turner

Vincent SETTLE....................................pg 350, 6 Apr 1854, Inv & Appr

men John, Sandy, boys Simon, Moses, girls Mary, Ann, women Eliza, Jane

Thornton LEACH..pg 358, 18 Dec 1854, Will

man Jeffery, who is willed to Nancy LEACH, is not to be sold

Benjamin ELLIOTT...pg 360, 5 Apr 1854, Will

old woman Amelia & her daughter Emily to daughter Susan CASLETT; man Sam & woman Suckey, to be emancipated, two of the servants derived from the former dec'd wife Maria

George W. CARTER...........................pg 368, 13 June 1855, Inv & Appr

Henry

John LOCKHART...pg 369, 15 Mar 1855, Sales

man Elias to Peter PRICE; woman Mary to Joseph D. LAWRENCE

William MILLER...pg 372, 3 Apr 1855, Will

Frederick, Willis, Robert, Denis, Baylis, Alsey, Lucy, Sarah, Amanda to wife Vina MILLER & at her death to children James L., Joseph W, & Mary MILLER; boy Afred to son Joseph W. MILLER; boy Frank to daughter Mary; boy Arthur to son Hampson M. MILLER

William WOODWARD ....pg 373, 20 Apr 1855, Inv & Appr

Maria, Jeny, Ann Maria, Sarah, Louisa; "These slaves and the three following children which are the increase of 2nd? woman was conveyed to E. FISH by William FISH by bill of sale dated"

Benjamin ELLIOTT ....pg 375, 3 May 1855, Inv & Appr

Robert, boy Jack, Sam, Sukey, Betsy & her son Jim, Emily & child Amelia, Martha & Aidesnia?, Dick 70, Thomas, George, Henry,

Sciatta?, Bill, John, Sue, Mary, Susan, Queen & child; Lucretia (in possession of Mrs. Lucretia THOMPSON)

Ruhamah M. BUCK .... pg 384, 1 Jan 1854 – 1 Jan 1855, Estate Acct

paid Maria Cooper

James R. ASH .... pg 386, 16 Jan 1854 - 1 Jan 1855, Estate Acct

Jane, Frank, Lucy hired to Charles? B. RUST, Ralph hired to J.R. RICHARDS, Jim hired to George ARMISTED, Susan hired to Alfred DEVAN___

Clarissa BARBEE .... pg 388, 19 July 1855, Inv & Appr

woman Ellen hired to Joseph BARBEE, Fanny & her child hired to John W. WINSBURRY, Maria & her child hired to John FIELDING, Agnes & her child at home, boy John at home, girl Hanna at N. RICHARDS, boy William at home, girl Sarah at home, girl Clarissa at N. RICHARDS, boy Alfred at home

Clarissa BARBEE .... pg 389, 20 July 1855, Sales

Agness hired to William GRANT

WILL BOOK Vol C
1856-1866

William CARSON.. pg 1, 4 May 1852, Will

    Thomas emancipated

Thornton LEACH.....................................pg 7, 28 July 1855, Inv & Appr

    man Jeffrey

William CARSON................................pg 12, 17 Mar 1856?, Inv & Appr

    Tom, Roberta & child, John, Louisa, Regina

William MILLER ....pg 15, 29 Oct 1855, Inv & Appr

    Frederick & wife, Willis, Bob, Dennis, Bailess, Arthur, Alfred, Frank,
    Lucy, Sarah, Amanda

Alex FINNELL Sr. .... pg 19, 20? Dec 1855, Sales

    men Ham, Elwood, Albert? hired to Ale & Hanson FINNELL, Hansy?
    hired to Hanson FINNELL

James Richard ASH .... pg 22, 5 Apr 1856, Inv & Appr

    Lydia 40, Tom 7, Sally 5, Haywood 3, Walker 1, Frank 55

.... pg 27, 5 Apr 1856, Sales

    slaves hired out: Frank, Lyida & 4 children to Nancy WAY

Samuel HOPEWELL ....pg 34, 13 Sept 1848, Will

    David, Adeline, Rachel, Henry Sr, Henry Jr., Arthelia, Thomas, James,
    Dodridge, Enoch, Richard, Bailes, Charlotte, Aramenta, Eliza to
    Louisa Elizabeth MOZINGO, Susan Ann BARGAR, Mary Adalaide
    CRISER & Virginia CRISER; Eliza & Rachel are not to be brought
    into the division, instead Eliza to Louisa Elizabeth MOZINGO &
    Rachel to Susan Ann BARGAR; woman Pamelia to Elizabeth CRISER

George G. TYLER, Prince William Co................ pg 36, 4 Mar 1855, Will

    negroes to daughters Annette & Hortensia

Samuel HOPEWELL ....pg 42, 11 Dec 1856, Inv & Appr

William, Henry, Charlot & 2 children, Enoch, Richard, Henry __, Athelia, James, Thomas, Pemelia

James R. ASH ....pg 44, 22 Jan – 31 Dec 1855, Gdn Acct

Lydia, woman, Frank, Jane & child

Samuel HOPEWELL ....pg 52, 16 Dec 1856, Sales

sold at public sale on 16 Feb 1857: Henry, Thomas to Eliza McDONALL, Richard, Arthelia to Richard COOPER, Enoch to William LILLIARD, Charlotte & children to B.P. CRISER

George TYLER .... pg 55, 1 Jan 1857 , Inv & Appr

Lewis 37, William 17, Jane 29, Lavinia 8, Dick 8, Francis 5, Landon 5, William 3, Julia 1

Benjamin ELLIOTT .... pg 58, 20 May 1855 - 22 July 1856, Estate Acct

"to T.F. BUCK negro Alfred for bringing negro girl Lucritia from Mrs. THOMPSON..." old Dick kept by ELLIOTT & CATLETT; Bob, Jack, Tom, Sukey & child, Henry to old Forsythe, Betsy & child, Sam, George, Emily & child, Scietto, Mary, Leonard, Jane, John, Susan

James R. ASH .... pg 65, 25 Dec 1856, Slave Inventory

old man Ralph; man Jim sold at public sale, boys Richard, Frank, girl Susan, Jane & child, Lucy & 2 children, woman Eliza; Louisa & child had small pox & remained with E. SHULL of Frederick Co; slaves hired out, & not named above, are embraced in the 1st inventory 19 Jan 1857

Hanson FINNELL .... pg 65, Mar 1857, Inv & Appr

Hannah, Edward, Ellen, Thomas, Ambrose

Elizabeth RUST.. pg 66, 16 July 1855, Will

little Lucy, woman Lily to grandson Bushrod RUST

J.W. McKAY...pg 67, 7 Aug 1847, Will

man Edmund to daughter Sarah F. McKAY

J.W. McKAY.. pg 67, 14 Jan 1855, 2nd Codicil

"...that my present wife Mary Ann had when I married her & has __ from her mother's estate of Colomea boy George, Sarah, Ellen, Israel, Ellias...wife shall have back again at my death..."

Samuel C. RICHARDSON .... pg 69, 5 Sept 1857, Inv & Appr

David, Anna & 2 children, Thornton, Sally, Judy, Robert, George, Matilda, Laura, Harrison, Mima, Anthony

Mary SHAMBAUGH .... pg 80, 13 Oct 1857, Will

boy John Reed to remain with sister Margaret as long as she lives, Margaret's 3 blacks are Jacob, Jonas, & Sarah "...John Reed shall serve the remainder of his time with Jacob & Rachael HOUSER & sister Margaret

Washington M. BOWMAN .... pg 85, no date, Will

slaves to be sold; in Court 19 Oct 1857

Alexander FINNELL Sr. ....
.... pg 86, 21 Dec 1855 – 1 May 1857, Estate Acct

Mary, a free negro; Albert, Elwood, Hamilton

Christopher KENDRICK ....
.... pg 90, 15 Aug 1853 – 25 Dec 1855, Estate Acct

Emily, Elizabeth, Neuman, Robert, Jim, Robin, Frank, Jane, Jim, Bill

Charles S. CHURCHILL...................... pg 100, 21 Sept 1857, Inv & Appr

Bill 18, Mary 43, John 28, old Mary

John W. McKAY................................. pg 102, 10 Aug 1857, Inv & Appr

Sarah 21, Eden 21, Elias 42, George 19, Israel 12

William WOODWARD ....
.... pg 112, 31 Mar 1855 – 31 Mar 1856, Estate Acct

paid free negro for cloth?

James R. ASH ....pg 122, 16 Jan – 31 Dec 1856, Gdn Acct

Jim, Louisa & child, Frank, Eliza

George W. CARTER.................pg 124, 5 Jan – 1 Dec 1856, Estate Acct

Henry

Alexander FERRELL .... pg 130, 3 Nov 1857, Sales

Elwood sold to MORRIS on 21 Sept 1857; Harry, Hamilton, Albert

Francis Wesley LEHEW ....
.... pg 134, 12 Aug 1853 – 4 Mar 1858, Gdn Acct

division of slaves; Sarah

Richard Castleman, a free man.........................pg 136, 24 Apr 1858, Will

"...if Miss Margaret SHAMBAUGH survives me, she shall not be dunned during her life time for any money or debt of any kind which she may owe me at the time of my death." "... sister's children: John R.C. Reed, Jacob H. Reed, Jonas H. Reed, & said Sarah Catharine Reed."

John W. McKAY... pg 137, 11 Aug 1857, Sale

women Sarah, Ellen, boy George to Mr. COOPER; boy Israel to Mr. MORRIS; Elias to J.W. JONES

John RUST devised to widow RUST ....
.... pg 142, 17 Aug 1857, Inv & Appr

girl Ann & child Alfred

Elizabeth RUST.. pg 144, 20 Aug 1857, Sale

woman Ann & child to Robert TURNER

James M. LAURENCE .... pg 148, 10 June 1858, Inv & Appr

Isaac, boy Harrison, girl Summerville

James R. ASH .... pg 162, 3 Apr 1856 - 1 Apr 1858, Estate Acct

Jim sold; Frank ran away, apprehended; Lydia & 4 children kept by Mrs. Nancy WAY, Ralph, Lucy, Eliza; *Alexandria Sentinal* ad for sale of slave Dec 1856; Jane, Ralph, Dick, Tom, Jane & child, Lucy & 2 children, Susan, Lydia & 4 children, Louisa & son

William LEARY .... pg 176, 24 July 1855, Will

girl Sarah to the heirs of daughter Mahala COLLINS; boy John to son William LEARY; girl Leah to daughter Jane BENNETT & her husband Richard BENNETT now in their possession; girl Eliza to son James M. LEARY; girl Caroline to son-in-law William BENNETT now in his possession; girl Julia to daughter Harriet RIDGEWAY & her husband William RIDGEWAY; girl Mary to daughter Maria HOFFMANN now in her possession; girl Ca_ander? to son Henry LEARY now in his possession; remainder of slaves to be divided between the children of daughter Sarah BENNETT, daughter Harriet & her husband William REDGEWAY, daughter Mahala COLLINS, son Henry LEARY, daughter Maria HOFFMAN, daughter Jane & her husband Richard BENNETT, son James M. LEARY, & son William LEARY

John S. ELLIOTT......................... pg 186, 1848 – 20 Dec 1857, Gdn Acct

negroes; division of Ben ELLIOTT's estate slaves; "...sale of negros Leonard & George, two of the slaves allotted to John S. ELLIOTT in the division of slaves of Ben ELLIOTT which two slaves were sold by WALKER to Benjamin ELLIOTT with the assent of John S. ELLIOTT dec'd on 2_ May 1856; women Sceatta?, & Sew__ having children during the years 1856 & 1857

W.H. HARRISON .... pg 192, 18 June 1858, Sales

woman & child; boy, 2 girls to R. COOPER

Isaac HARRISON .... pg 200, 18 Aug 1858, Sales

boy Davy, girl Ailey to R. COOPER; boy Charlie to R.B. BRASHEAR; boys Dick, Sam, girl, woman Easter, man Jim to T.S. SWA__

Harriet M. BOWEN .... pg 204, 23 Nov 1858, Inv & Appr

Baalis, Jim, Caroline, Strother, Fanny, Margaret & 2 children

Samuel C. RICHARDSON .... pg 214, 14 Dec 1858, Sales

boys Harrison, Thornton to Richard COOPER; boy Robert to S.P. WALKENS; girl Laura to A.S. GRIGSBY; girl Sally to W.B. BRAWNER

George G. TYLER .... pg 220, 1 Jan – 13 Dec 1857, Estate Acct

man Bill; free negro Alexander; Bill sold

Samuel C. RICHARDSON ....
....pg 222, 28 July 1857 – 15 June 1858, Adm Acct

boy Thornton

Frances C.N. BROWN .... pg 232, 27 Dec 1858, Inv & Appr

Harry, Lewis, Sarah, Caroline, Kate

Christopher Johnston .... pg 234, 8 Feb 1859, Inv & Appr

Christopher Johnston, a free man

Harriet M. BOWEN .... pg 239, 27 Dec 1858, Div of Slaves

Lot 1) Baalis, Mary to James BOWEN; Lot 2) Strother, William to J.H.
JAMESON; Lot 3) Margaret, Grandison to A.J. BOWEN; Lot 4)
Elizabeth, Kate to J.H. WHEATLY; Lot 5) Bob to J.W. FIELDS; Lot
6) Caroline, Fanny to Walter BOWEN

S.J. BRAWNER? .... pg 241, 22 Feb 1859, Inv & Appr

boy Charley

Bush KEELER .... pg 246, 1 Dec 1855 - 21 Jan 1857, Estate Acct

girl

Daniel CLOUD .... pg 252, 14 June 1856 – 1 May 1858, Estate Acct

woman Maria

Mordicai CLOUD .... pg 256, 11 July 1855, Will

Peter, Ann, Louisa to wife Rebecca B. CLOUD

William LEWIN .... pg 258, 29 Jan 1858, Will

Miner, Charles, Reason, Julie Ann, Tim to wife Polly Ann; the
remainder of slaves to be sold; "...David Mitchell a free man of color
if he may desire to take or buy his wife Nancy and her youngest
child..."

A. FINNELL ....pg 261, 19 July 1858, Sales

Albert to John JETT; Harry to C._. HANCOCK; Hamilton to Samuel B. GARDNER; Clarinda? & children to J.B. PETTY

Nimrod MASSIE...................pg 268, Mar 1855 - 31 ___ 1857, Estate Acct

burial of child; old Clara, Titus 50, Turner 42, Mildsen? 39 & 3 children, Caroline 37 & 2 children; John 17, Moses 16, Tom 14, John 15, Jacob 12, Margaret 15, Sally

Clarissa BARBEE .... pg 280, June 1855 - 21 Deb 1857, Estate Acct

2 children boarded by Cornelius RICKARDS; Ellen who ran off, Maria & child, Agnes, Fanny, John, Harriett

James R. ASH .... pg 284, 16 Sept 1858 – 17 Feb 1859, Estate Acct

Lucy's child; Louisa & children, Lucy died, Eliza & child, Jane & children, Lydia & 4 children; Jim, Ralph, Frank, Richard, boy Frank, Tom, Susan

Daniel CLOUD .... pg 288, 1 May 1858 – 1 Jan 1859, Estate Acct

Maria

Samuel HOPEWELL ....pg 294, 15 Dec 1836 - 16 June 1857, Estate Acct

slaves sold, boy James sold; Henry

William RICHARDSON.........................pg 297, 6 Dec 1859, Inv & Appr

Hannah 61, Lewis 60, Sinah 53 & sons Henry 19 & Bob 16; Henry 46, Eliza 40 & child Amelia 1; Jim 37, Francis 32 & children Clara 6, Simon 4 & Hannah; Sylvia 31 & children Alia 10, Charlie 12, Mary 7, & Henry 4; Will 29, Lottie 25 & children Cornelia 7, Frank 5 & Polly 3; Lucinda 23 & son Addeson 1; Rachael 16, Adam 16, Eve 12, Cuffie 10, Jeminie 8, Mary 4

John F. BOYD.......................................pg 311, 8 June 1860, Inv & Appr

men Daniel, Dennis, woman Linda, boy Buley, girls Ann, Lucy, Charlotte, boy Daniel, girls Charity, Cathleen, boys Alfred, Taylor

William LEWIN...................................... pg 319, Aug 1859, Inv & Appr

Nancy & child, Thomas 20, Isaac 15, Melville 13, Ann Maria 10

William LEWIN .... pg 321, no date, per Will

bequeathed to Widow: Julia Ann 18, Amanda Jane 8 months, Alex 70, Minor 47, Charles 33, Reason 29, James 7

Mrs. Mary FINNELL .... pg 328, 6 June 1860, Inv & Appr

girl Ellen, Hannah & 3 children Thomas, Ambrose, & Benton; Edward

J.B. EARLE... pg 329, 9 Sept 1860, Inv & Appr

Israel, Charlotte & 4 children Elizabeth, Wesley, Caroline, & Joseph; Eliza, Laura, Mary, Ann, George, Moses, Tom, Clary, Blenda & 3 children Amos, James, & Clary; Mack, Charles, Harriet & child Anna, Robert, Eliza & child Stephen A. Douglass, Alfred, Clayton, Adalaid, Nancy, Frank, Ann, Bartlett, George Blair, Frank Burns, Ben, Peter, Ambrose, Calvin, Willis, Jack, Henry

William GRANT .... pg 347, 29 Aug 1860, Inv & Appr

Kitty 64, Malinda 41, Charles 34, Land__ 34, Sarah 33 & child, Henry 25, Lewis 11, Mary 8?, George, 7

William LEWIN.. pg 356, 27 Jan 1859, Sales

man Thomas, girl Ann Maria to Thomas GOLDEN; girl Melvilla to C.B. HANCOCK; Nancy & child to David MITCHELL; Isaac sold 24 Aug 1860 to John SIBERT

Margaret SHAMBAUGH.................................... pg 358, 5 Jan 1860, Will

2 colored boys & a girl, Jacob H. Reed, Jonas H. Reed, & Sarah C. Reed who I raised "…after my death Jonas H. Reed, & Sarah C. Reed shall be at liberty and free..J.H. HOUSER to be their guardian"

James R. ASH .... pg 364, 10 Aug 1859 – 5 Jan 1860, Admin Acct

slaves sold

Harriet M. BOWEN ......pg 366, 25 Nov 1858 - 27 Dec 1859 Admin Acct

Thornton, Baalis, Fanny, Strother

Daniel CLOUD ....pg 368, 18 July 1859 – 5 Sept 1860, Admin Acct

Maria

Mary C.J. CARSON .... pg 372, 9 Feb 1857 – 1 Jan 1858, Gdn Acct

Steve at trial & in jail; Stephen sold?, Bill, Lucinda

Mordicai CLOUD .... pg 389, 21 June 1859 – 18 June 1860, Exec Acct

servants

Joshua A. McKAY .... pg 404, 16 July 1861, Will

Washington Wells, a free man, to have the house occupied by George WAY

James E. BEATY .... pg 394, 6 Dec 1858 – 15 Sept 1859, Admin Acct

Jane, James died

Marcus T. BUCK .... pg 406, 1 Mar 1860, List

Notes & Accounts due Marcus T. BUCK which have been placed in the hands of Thomas _. ASHBY his curator by J.B. LEHEW

(pg 424) Alfred 40, Dennis 35, Margaret 29, Robert 9, Elgera? 5, Ben 3, Maria 1

William BEATY .... pg 426, 14 Sept 1861, Inv & Appr

girls Mary Ann, Julia, Jane, boys Jack, Thomas William, woman & child

William LEVIN .... pg 428, 25 Aug 1859 – 31 Dec 1860, Exec Acct

Nancy & child purchased by David MITCHELL; slaves purchased by Thomas GOLDER; slave purchased by C.B. HANCOCK; slaves purchased by Peyton STINSON

Jacob VANNORT .... pg 437, 20 Mar 1858, Will

servants to be sold

Rachal WOODWARD .... pg 438, 3 Jan 1862, Inv & Appr

woman 31 & child age 2, both considered unsound

.... pg 439, 20 Jan 1862, Inv & Appr

woman Sidney, boys Jack, Henry

Jacob VANNORT .... pg 445, Feb 1862, Inv & Appr

Sarah 12 in July 1861, Martha 11 in June 1861, Thornton 10 in June 1861, Tom 9 in Feb 1861

Daniel CLOUD .... pg 449, 5 Sept 1860 - 8 Dec 1861, Adm Acct

Mary Pierce

William RICHARDSON ...... pg 456, Dec 1859 - 30 Dec 1860, Adm Acct

3 servants at Mt. Jackson; servants in Surry?; boy Bob sold to S.W. BOWMAN of Harrisonburg

Rachael KENNER .... pg 462, 22 Sept 1858 - 22 July 1859, Adm Acct

Caroline & 3 children, girl Betty, boy Thornton, girl Leantha?

Marcus T. BUCK .... pg 464, 9 Mar 1860 – 1 Mar 1861, Comm Acct

servants

William BEATY .... pg 466, 12 Apr 1862, Bonds & Notes

Clarissa & 2 children to John B. PETTY

Manly T. WHEATLEY .... pg 469, 6 Feb 1862, Inv & App

Parlour 25, Jonas 14, Catharine 22 & child age 1, Bell 13, Mary Ann 40

Robert L. McKAY .... pg 471, 3 Oct 1860, Will

"...to my wife Jane R. all the slaves she possessed when we were married, and all those inherited since that time from her fathers estate both of which have been transferred to her by my deed..."

Joseph T. KENNER .... pg 475, 24 Aug 1862, Will

old Vina to be free. Fenton to be free after serving my brother Thomas 10 years; Frederick belonging to James R. RICHARDS to be paid

Thomas BUCK, Sr. .... pg 476, 27 Oct 1855, Will

Ann, Philip, Harriet to wife; girl Harriet to granddaughter Amelia Ann BUCK wife of J.N.? BUCK; old woman Ann to son John G. BUCK

Thomas BUCK, Sr. ....pg 477, 21 Feb 1857, 2nd Codicil

"...boy Philip to son Thomas C. BUCK, but if he is not willing to go to Missouri that John G. BUCK may keep him..."

John Gill BUCK ....pg 483, 30 Dec 1862, Inv & Appr

Eveline 29, Charles 10, Dawson 6, Mary 23, Jim 25

Jacob VANNORT ....pg 487, 29 Dec 1862, Inv & Appr

Sarah 13 in July 1862, Martha 12 in June 1862, Thornton 11 in June 1862, Tom 9 in Feb 1862

....pg 487, 29 Dec 1862, Sales

Sarah 13 to David E. ALMOND, Martha 12 to A.R. BOONE, Thornton 11 to Alfred VANNORT, Tom 9 to S.M.? BOWMAN

Charles M. GREEN ....pg 488, 29 Oct 1962. Inv & Appr

Sallie 42, Margaret 17, Jacob 14, Russel 12, Emily 26 & child, Eveline 40, Mary Louisa 9, C_oney 6, Elias 3, Ive Rines 40, Lucy 13; Archer 5 & Isaac 20 belongs to Mr. GREEN

William ROBINSON ....pg 495, 7 Nov 1854, Will

girl Caroline to granddaughter Ann POMEROY; boy Alfred to son John ROBINSON; remaining negroes to sons Benjamin ROBINSON & Vincent ROBINSON

William RICHARDSON......pg 500, 1 Jan 1861 – 5 Apr 1862, Adm Acct

Will

Marcus T. BUCK ....pg 504, 1 Jan 1862 – 1 Jan 1863, Comm Acct

Alfred

William BEATY ....pg 506, 1 Sept 1861 – 21 June 1862, Adm Acct

Ellen

George G. TYLER ....pg 508, 18 Jan 1858 – 1 Jan 1861, Estate Acct

Lewis died

Elizabeth CRISER...............................pg 518, 22 Sept 1863, Inv & Appr

old Pemmy, old Will

Jacob McKAY ....pg 522, Sept 1852 – Aug 1861, Exec Acct

slaves appraised 1 Aug 1854 (date of the death of the widow): Mary to John G. BUCK, Eliza & child to Thomas B. McKAY, Amanda to Robert S. McKAY, Nancy & John to Joshua A. McKAY

Ann LEHEW .... pg 528, 3 Jan 1861, Will

Jane, Scatta to son Jonathan B. LEHEW

Robert L. McKAY.................................pg 531, 26 Dec 1862, Inv & Appr

man Alf, Harrison, woman May Ann, Amanda

Jacob VANNORT .... pg 544, 3 Mar 1863 – 1 July 1864, Exec Acct

Sarah; Martha sold to A.R. BOONE on 29 Dec 1862; Thornton sold to Alfred VANNORT

Marcus T. BUCK .... pg 547, 27 Dec 1862 – 21 July 1863, Adm Acct

Alf; Margaret & children sold

Charles M. GREEN.........pg 548, 1 Dec 1862 – 26 Dec 1863, Estate Acct

Joe

Marcus C. RICHARDSON .... pg 558, 17 May 1863, Will

slaves to be divided among children: Elizabeth E.R. FINNY, John C. RICHARDSON, Susan A. HITE wife of P.Y. HITE, Lucie I. CHRISMAN wife of Joseph M. CHRISMAN, Marcus F. RICHARDSON, & Mary V. RICHARDSON, & the children of son Samuel C. RICHARDSON dec'd; Maria & her daughter Martha to choose own masters; children of female slaves are not to be separated from their mothers

Joshua A. McKAY .... pg 576, 19 Nov 1863 - 15 Sept 1864, Exec Acct

servants

Hanson FENNELL.........pg 597, 30 Apr 1857 - 20 Dec 1865, Estate Acct

Edmund

Charles H. GREEN .... pg 612, 1 Dec 1862 – 3 Feb 1866, Admin Acct

Joe, Emily

Robert B. ASHBY ....pg 1, 9 Aug 1839, Will

negroes to daughter Mary Ann ASHBY, to be hired out

....pg 6, Aug 1838 - 25 June 1840, Exec Acct

George, Sarah, man Oliver

Ezekiel WHITE......................................pg 10, 18 Mar 1863, Inv & Appr

girl Eleanor, Sydney & child

.... pg 11, 19 Apr 1843, Sales

Sydney & child, girl Ellen to James R. RICHARDS

James SINCLAIR, Frederick Co...................... pg 15, 28 May 1824, Will

Henry, Stephen & his wife Lydia to choose next owner; Diner to wife
Ann SINCLAIR to be free at her death

Sydney & child, girl Ellen to James R. RICHARDS

Robert B. ASHBY .... pg 16, 1 July 1840 – 20 Dec 1842, Exec Acct

Ned

Ezekiel WHITE ....pg 22, 11 Sept 1839, Will

boy John to daughter Sary Ann; woman Sal to choose her own master;
remaining negroes to be sold

Isaac B. CLOUD .... pg 26, 2 Dec 1846, Will

servants to wife Amelia A. CLOUD but can be sold if necessary

James SINCLAIR...............pg 27, 2 Sept 1844 – 30 Aug 1847, Adm Acct

Martha, Malinda & 3 children sold to A.S. TIDBALL, Joseph, James,
Maria sold to J.R. RICHARDS; Martha taken to Georgetown for his
own service by Jacob G. SMOOT, Admin

Isaac B. CLOUD .... pg 30, 4 Sept 1846, Inv & Appr

Vina 45, Ashby 37, Matilda 28, Enoch 29, John 23, Mary 18, Smith 17, Elizabeth 15, Meredith 10, Martha 8, Robert 5, Arthur 7, Sally 6, Alexander 5, Henry 3, Daniel infant

.... pg 33, 1 __ 1847 - 1 Sept 1851, Exec Acct

Frederick

.... pg 42, 1 Sept 1852 – 1 Sept 1853, Exec Acct

Charlie

.... pg 45, 26 May 1855, Inv & Appr

Ashby, Matilda, Enoch, Meredith, Arthur, Robert, Alexander, Henry, Daniel, Sally, Joseph, Julias, Eli

....pg 55, 1 Sept 1853 – 1 Aug 1855, Exec Acct

girl Elizabeth, Patty, woman Harriet, Adam, Milly, Arthur, Bob, Sally

....pg 69, 1 Sept 1855 – 3 July 1856, Exec Acct

Matilda, Toliver, Enoch, Robert, Sally

.... pg 71, 1 Sept 1856 – 1 Jan 1858, Exec Acct

sale of slaves; "...the personal estate (other than the slaves) was not sufficient to pay the debts...(and then to reserve the slaves for division) the two brothers Isaac Newton CLOUD and Thomas William CLOUD each advanced..."

William G. BEATY................. pg 75, 1 Jan 1863 - 1 Jan 1865, Adm Acct

girl, Ellen & children

Isaac N. BUCK.. pg 86, 25 Jan 1854, Will

slaves to wife Janet W?. BUCK; Dennis, Susan, Ann, Johnson & child Laura to children by first marriage: Marcus T. BUCK, Mary C. BUCK, Catherine E. BLAKEMAN formerlyCatherine E. BUCK, & Susan R. BUCK; slaves at death of Janet W.? BUCK to the children by last marriage

Wilson N. MELLON .... pg 100, 18 May 1880, Inv & Appr

negroes

44

"...to Mary colored girl raised by us known by the name of Mary Fristoe but bound to M.F.? FRISTOE by the name of Mary Barbee..."

certain household staff to Mrs. Annie E. McKAY

R., 9; Robert B., 43; Thomas,
39; William R., 9
Askins: Phil, 26; Philip, 23
Athalinda, 5
Athelia, 32

Baalis, 3, 5, 9, 13, 35, 36, 38
Bailes, 2, 31
Bailess, 31
BAKER: Eliza, 21; Ewell, 15;
Samuel, 21
Barbee: Mary, 45
BARBEE: Clarissa, 29, 37;
Joseph, 29
BARGAR: Susan Ann, 31
Bartlett, 38
BAYARLY: Richard, 21
Baylis, 28
BEALE: Elizabeth, 9; Giles C.,
9; Joseph C., 9; Nancy, 8
BEATY: James E., 39;
William, 21, 39, 40, 41;
William G., 44
Bebee: Gilbert, 15
Bee: Gilbert B, 15, 20
Bell, 40
Ben, 3, 5, 7, 9, 11, 13, 14, 16,
17, 21, 23, 24, 26, 38, 39
Benjamin, 2, 17
BENNETT: Jane, 35; Richard,
35; Sarah, 35
Benton, 38
BERKELY: Benjamin F., 7
Betsy, 2, 8, 25, 28, 32
Betty, 10, 11, 17, 21, 23, 24, 40
Bill, 10, 16, 17, 18, 27, 29, 33,
36, 39
Billy, 21
BLACKMAN: T.L., 10
BLACKMORE: Letitia, 7
BLACKWOOD: James, 7;
Levi, 7; Massy, 7; Richard, 7;
Thomas, 7, 9; William, 7

Blair: George, 38
BLAKEMAN: Catherine E., 44
Blenda, 38
Bob, 12, 16, 23, 24, 31, 32, 36,
37, 40, 44
BOONE: A.R., 41, 42
BORDEN: Philip, 21
BOWEN: A.J., 36; Ann Mariah,
22; Harriet M., 35, 36, 38;
James, 2, 3, 5, 9, 13, 36;
Mrs., 5, 13; W., 16, 24;
Walter, 13, 19, 36
BOWMAN: S.M., 41; S.W., 40;
Washington M., 33
BOYD: John F., 37
BRASHEAR: R.B., 25, 35
BRAWNER: S.J., 36; W.B., 35
Broaddus, 16
BROADUS: John W.F., 22
BROWN: Frances C.N., 36;
James, 2; Richard, 17;
Thomas, 12
BROWNING: Joseph, 5;
Winifred, 1, 5
BRUIN: Joseph, 26
BRYARLY: Richard, 23
Buck, 15, 20
BUCK: Amelia Ann, 40; Capt.
Thomas, 11, 26; Catharine,
22; Catherine E., 44; Charles,
11, 24; Eliza, 11, 24; Isaac
N., 44; J.N., 40; Janet W., 44;
John, 11; John B., 24; John
G., 11, 40, 41, 42; John Gill,
41; Marcus, 22; Marcus C.,
15, 21; Marcus T., 39, 40, 41,
42, 44; Mary, 22; Mary C.,
44; Ruhamah, 7; Ruhamah
M., 23, 26, 29; Samuel, 11;
Sarah, 11; Sarah J., 24;
Susan, 22; Susan R., 44; T.F.,
32; Thomas, 7, 11, 14, 16,
21, 40, 41; Thomas C., 41

BUCKLEY: Benjamin T., 2, 3
Bud, 15, 20
Buley, 37
Burns: Frank, 38
BURNS: J.S., 16

C_oney, 41
CAIN: Hannah, 4
CALMES: Henrietta, 7
Calvin, 22, 25, 38
CANON: John, 21
Caraneter, 35
Caroline, 2, 6, 8, 12, 16, 17, 22, 35, 36, 37, 38, 40, 41
CARPER: James, 15
CARSON: Mary C.J., 39; William, 31
CARTER: George W., 28, 34; W.A., 24
CASE: James, 4; Margaret, 4; Mary Ann, 4, 7; Robert B., 4
CASLETT: Susan, 28
Castleman: Richard, 34
Catharine, 17, 20, 22, 23, 24, 40
Cathleen, 37
CATLETT, 32; Alexander, 16; Peter, 13
Charity, 1, 2, 37
Charles, 2, 5, 10, 11, 17, 23, 25, 26, 36, 38, 41
Charley, 36
Charlie, 35, 37, 44
Charlot, 32
Charlotte, 2, 6, 12, 17, 20, 21, 22, 23, 24, 25, 31, 32, 37, 38
Chartel, 17
Chasity, 2
CHENSMITH: A.G., 27
China, 10
CHRISMAN: Joseph M., 42; Lucie I., 42
Churchill, 17; Lewis Charles, 17

CHURCHILL: Charles, 17, 18; Charles S., 33; John, 17, 24; Margaret, 24; Susan, 24
Clara, 2, 3, 13, 37
Clarinda, 37
Clarissa, 8, 10, 11, 29, 40
CLARK: W., 16
Clary, 5, 9, 15, 38
Clayton, 38
Cleg__, 2
CLINE: J.M., 16
CLOUD: Amalia A., 43; Daniel, 36, 37, 38, 40; Isaac B., 43, 44; M., 16; Mordicai, 27, 36, 39; Newton, 44; Rebecca B., 36; Thomas William, 44
COCK: James, 3
COLLINS: Mahala, 35
COMPTON: Dorea, 12; Elias E., 4; Elizabeth E., 4; John, 4, 6, 12; John A., 4; Laura G., 4; Mary Ann C., 4; Peggy C., 4; William C., 4
CONRAD: William, 16; William S., 20, 26
COOK: Giles, 15, 27; William, 8, 9, 12, 15
COONRAD: James, 5; Joseph, 5
Cooper: Maria, 23, 29
COOPER: Mr., 34; R., 35; Richard, 32, 35
Cornelia, 16, 37
CRABILL: Abed, 14
CRISER: B.P., 32; Elizabeth, 31, 41; Mary Adalaide, 31; Virginia, 31
CROSS: J., 15; James, 5, 19, 24
Cuddelah: Frances, 8
Cuffie, 37

Dallas, 20

49

50

FINNELL Sr.: Alex, 31;
  Alexander, 33
FINNY: Elizabeth E.R., 42
FISH: E., 28; William, 28
FLEMMING: Andrew, 4
Flora, 15, 20
Florinda, 5
FOLEY: Rachel, 14; Selby, 14,
  17, 23
Forsythe, 32
Frances, 10, 12, 25
Francis, 32, 37
Frank, 3, 7, 10, 12, 16, 19, 23,
  24, 26, 28, 29, 31, 32, 33, 34,
  37, 38
Frederick, 5, 16, 17, 28, 31, 40,
  44
Fristoe: Mary, 45
FRISTOE: Elizabeth, 15; Lucy,
  15; M.F., 45; Priscilla, 15;
  Sarah, 15; Sarah E., 45; Silas,
  15; Susan, 15
FRISTOE, Jr.: William, 15
FUNKHOUSER: Daniel, 21;
  Isaac, 21; Jacob, 21; Mary,
  21; William D., 21
FUNSTEN: A.R., 13; O.R., 20,
  26

GARDNER: John B., **27**; Mrs.
  E., 8; Rebecca, 25; S.B., 25;
  Samuel, 3, 8, 10, 11, 14;
  Samuel B., 10, 25, 37; Sarah
  C., 25, **27**
GATEWOOD: Chancy, 9
General, 20
General Henry Lee, 15
Genitta, 11
George, 2, 6, 7, 8, 9, 10, 11, 12,
  17, 18, 19, 20, 21, 22, 23, 24,
  28, 32, 33, 34, 35, 38, 43
Gilbert, 15
Ginny, 15

GLASSCOCK: John, 19
GOLDEN: Thomas, 38
GOLDER: Thomas, 39
Gordan, 5
Grandison, 36
Granison, 16
GRANT: Nancy, 4, 6; William,
  29, 38
Grayson, 16
GREEN: Charles H., 42;
  Charles M., 41, 42
Grend__, 23
GRIGSBY: A.S., 35
Gustavus, 21, 25, 26
GUTHRIDGE: Elijah, 5;
  Elizabeth, 1, 5

HADDON: Laura G., 4
Haidenia, 17
HALL: John W., 8; M.L., 9;
  Richard F., 8; Richard T., 9
Ham, 31
Hamilton, 6, 7, 9, 25, 33, 34, 37
Hampson, 3
HANCOCK: C., 37; C.B., 38,
  39
HAND: William B., 20
Haner, 1
Hanna, 29
Hannah, 1, 2, 3, 4, 6, 14, 15, 16,
  17, 23, 26, 32, 37, 38
Hanner, 19
HANSBROUGH: John, 21;
  Lucy, 1, 21; Margaret, 1, 2;
  Mary W., 21; Presley, 1, 21,
  25, 26; Sarah, 1, 2
Hansy, 31
Harlow, 26; Mary, 15, 20, 26
Harret, 15
Harriet, 7, 8, 10, 11, 16, 21, 23,
  25, 26, 27, 38, 40, 44
Harriett, 7, 8, 12, 14, 37
Harrison, 10, 33, 34, 35, 42

HARRISON: Isaac, 8, 21, 23, 35; W.H., 35
Harry, 7, 9, 11, 34, 36, 37
Hatty, 4
HAYNIE: Margaret, 16
Haywood, 31
HEADLEY: James, 1; William, 1, 2
HEADLY: James, 5; Newton, 1; William, 5, 10
HEADLY Jr.: William, 5
Henny, 17, 18
Henny Ash, 17
Henretta, 9
Henrietta, 7, 9
Henry, 1, 2, 3, 5, 6, 8, 17, 18, 21, 22, 23, 24, 28, 31, 32, 34, 37, 38, 39, 43, 44
Hester, 20
HICKS: T.V., 27
HINKELY: Mary Ann C., 4
Hirena, 2
HITE: John, 7, 9, 12; P.Y., 42; Susan A., 42
HOFFMAN: Maria, 35
HOFFMANN: Maria, 35
HOPEWELL: Samuel, 31, 32, 37; William, 6, 7, 9, 12, 25
HOUSER: J.H., 38; Jacob, 33; Rachael, 33
Howard, 17
HOWELL: Sampson, 8
HUNT: Thomas, 25

Iris, 3, 7, 10, 12, 19
Isaac, 4, 7, 9, 14, 34, 37, 38, 41
Israel, 33, 34, 38
Ive, 41

Jack, 4, 6, 7, 8, 10, 26, 28, 32, 38, 39
Jackson, 11
JACKSON: John R., 19, 27

Jacob, 1, 2, 5, 16, 17, 23, 27, 33, 37, 41
JACOBS: Newman M., 27
James, 1, 2, 3, 4, 5, 6, 7, 9, 13, 14, 15, 21, 24, 25, 31, 32, 37, 38, 39, 43
JAMESON: J.H., 36
Jane, 7, 16, 19, 23, 25, 26, 27, 28, 29, 32, 33, 34, 37, 39, 42
Janella, 11
Janny, 1, 3
Jany, 1
Jeff, 5, 9, 13
Jeffers, 3
Jefferson, 2, 6, 7, 9
Jeffery, 28
Jeffrey, 10, 14, 31
Jeminie, 37
Jeny, 2, 21, 28
Jeremiah, 22, 23
Jerry, 6, 27
Jesse, 23, 26
Jetson, 4, 7
JETT: John, 37
Jim, 4, 5, 8, 9, 12, 13, 16, 17, 19, 23, 24, 25, 26, 28, 29, 32, 33, 34, 35, 37, 41
Joe, 6, 8, 10, 11, 15, 21, 42
John, 1, 2, 8, 13, 15, 19, 21, 22, 23, 24, 25, 27, 28, 29, 31, 32, 33, 35, 37, 42, 43, 44
JOHN: Thomas, 17, 20, 21, 24
Johnson, 44
JOHNSON: William R., 16
Johnston: Christopher, 36
JOHNSTON: P., 16
JOLLIFFE: John, 23
Jonas, 33, 40
Jones: Susan, 26
JONES: J.W., 34; Joel W., 21
Jordan, 13, 18
Joseph, 15, 38, 43, 44
Joshua, 23

Josiah, 23
Judah, 6
Judy, 14, 16, 21, 33
Julia, 11, 35, 39
Julia Ann, 38
Julias, 44
Julie Ann, 36

Kate, 3, 36
KEELER: Bush, 36
KENDRICK: C., 10;
  Christopher, 15, 16, 19, 24,
  26, 33; Jacob, 5; John, 1;
  Lucinda, 1; Lucy, 5; Mrs.,
  24; Rebeca, 1; Rebecca, 5;
  William S., 19
KENDRICKS: C., 12
KENNER: Joseph, 20; Joseph
  T., 40; Rachael, 40; W.H., 8
KING: August, 12; M.L., 9;
  Maria Louisa, 5; Mary, 5;
  Mrs., 6; Summerville, 5;
  Virlinda, 12; William A., 5,
  6, 9, 12
Kitty, 6, 25, 38
KNISALY: R., 10

LAKE: Harvey, 8; Johnston, 8;
  Mildred, 8; Thomas, 9
LAN_ER: Sarah, 1
Land__, 38
Landon, 20, 23, 32
Laura, 33, 35, 38, 44
LAURENCE: James M., 34
Lavina, 6
Lavinia, 32
LAWLER: Sarah, 5; Thomas, 5
LAWRENCE: Alcinda Ann,
  14; James M., 14; Jane, 6;
  Joseph D., 28; Lewis, 9;
  Polly, 4, 6; Susan, 6

LEACH: John, 24; Mary, 10;
  Nancy, 28; Thornton, 14, 28,
  31
Leah, 35
Leantha, 40
LEARY: Henry, 35; James M.,
  35; William, 35
Lee: General, 20; Henry, 15
LEHEW: Ann, 19, 20, 42; Ann
  Elizabeth, 22, 25; Charles
  Edwin, 20, 21, 25; Edwin,
  22; Elizabeth, 20, 21; Francis
  Weley, 34; Francis Wesley,
  21, 22, 25; Francis Wesly,
  20; J.B., 39; Jonathan B., 19,
  22, 42
Leonard, 32, 35
Letty, 19, 22
LEVIN: William, 39
Levina, 12
LEWIN: William, 8, 36, 37, 38
Lewis, 4, 11, 13, 14, 15, 16, 17,
  18, 19, 32, 36, 37, 38, 41
Lewy, 16
Lidda, 8
Liddy, 11
LILLIARD: William, 32
Lily, 32
Linda, 37
Lindsey, 17
LIPSCOMB: Robert, 8
LOCHART: M.A., 6; Mary
  Ann, 6
LOCKHART: John, 26, 28
LONG: R.S., 9
Lottie, 37
Lotty, 15
Louisa, 5, 7, 9, 10, 12, 13, 14,
  16, 17, 18, 19, 20, 22, 23, 24,
  26, 28, 31, 32, 33, 34, 36, 37
Louiza, 3, 19
Lucinda, 2, 3, 5, 8, 9, 11, 13,
  14, 17, 37, 39

Lucretia, 29
Lucritia, 32
Lucy, 3, 4, 5, 6, 7, 9, 12, 13, 16,
  19, 26, 27, 28, 29, 31, 32, 34,
  37, 41
Luesa, 19
Lydia, 3, 7, 8, 10, 12, 17, 19,
  21, 23, 25, 27, 31, 32, 34, 37,
  43

Mack, 38
Mahala, 15
Malinda, 12, 17, 23, 38, 43
MANCH: James, 24
Manda, 28
Manuel, 3, 16
Margaret, 2, 5, 7, 9, 13, 23, 35,
  36, 37, 39, 41, 42
Margarett, 23
Maria, 7, 8, 10, 11, 14, 19, 20,
  21, 22, 23, 25, 26, 28, 29, 36,
  37, 38, 39, 42, 43
Mariah, 1, 2, 6, 22, 23
Marian, 8
Mariga, 6
Mariza, 4
Marlbrough, 17
MARSHALL: Francis, 7, 8, 11
Martha, 5, 9, 11, 17, 20, 24, 26,
  27, 28, 40, 41, 42, 43, 44
Marthina, 4, 6
Martin, 9, 23, 25
Mary, 1, 2, 3, 5, 6, 9, 10, 13, 15,
  16, 17, 18, 19, 20, 21, 22, 23,
  24, 25, 26, 27, 28, 29, 32, 33,
  35, 36, 37, 38, 40, 41, 42, 44,
  45
Mary Ann, 17, 20, 23, 24, 39,
  40
Mary Elizabeth, 17
Mary Louisa, 41
Mary Susan, 9
Mason, 1

MASON: James W., 17; Marth,
  8
MASSIE: Franklin H., 28;
  Franklin W., 27; George T.,
  19; Nimrod, 37
Matalda, 9
Matilda, 4, 6, 7, 9, 12, 15, 20,
  25, 33, 44
May Agnes, 17
May Ann, 42
McCARTNEY: Joseph, 8
McCUBBIN: Frances, 8
McDANIEL: John, 22
McDONALD: John, 25, 27
McDONALL: Eliza, 32
McKAY: Annie E., 45;
  Elizabeth, 11; J., 9; J.W., 32,
  33; Jacob, 24, 28, 42; Jane
  R., 40; Jesse H., 24, 45; John,
  12; John W., 33, 34; Joshua
  A., 39, 42; Nancy, 11; Nancy
  A., 24; Oscar, 24; R.S., 24;
  Robert, 11; Robert L., 40, 42;
  Robert S., 42; Sarah F., 32;
  Thomas, 24; Thomas B., 42;
  William B., 24
McPHERSON: Nancy, 8
MEADE: John W., 17
Melinda, 6, 21
MELLON: Wilson N., 44
Melvilla, 38
Melville, 37
MENIFER: A., 12, 25
Meredith, 23, 44
Mildred, 16, 19, 24, 26
Mildsen, 37
MILLAR: John W., 5; Mary, 5
MILLER: Hampson M., 28;
  James L., 28; John, 19;
  Joseph W., 28; Mary, 1, 28;
  Vina, 28; William, 28, 31
Milley, 10, 15
Milly, 4, 7, 8, 11, 28, 44

Milton, 18
Mima, 33
Min_, 8
Miner, 36
Minor, 8, 38
Mirah, 4
Mitchell: David, 36
MITCHELL: David, 38, 39
MONROE: Ann, 10; Eliza, 10;
  Ethelinda, 10; George, 10;
  John, 10; Thomas, 10;
  William, 10, 14
Morgan, 5
MORRIS, 34; Mr., 34
Moses, 1, 6, 18, 23, 24, 27, 28,
  37, 38
MOZINGO: Louisa Elizabeth,
  31
MURPHY: Ab__, 4; Alcinda,
  4; Alexander, 14, 15;
  Alsinda, 6; Betsy, 4, 6;
  Elizabeth, 4, 6, 14; Grafton,
  15; John Lewis, 14; Mary, 8
MURRELL: John, 23
MYERS: Samuel, 8

Nancy, 1, 2, 3, 8, 12, 16, 19, 23,
  27, 36, 37, 38, 39, 42
Nannie, 28
Nanny, 2
Ned, 43
Nelly, 11
Nelson, 17
Neuman, 33
NEUMAN: Catharine, 10;
  Sarah, 10
Newman, 24, 26
Newton, 19, 20, 21, 22, 25

O'Dalphin, 6
Oliver, 43
OLIVER: M., 8
OVERALL: Isaac, 10

P__ER: John, 16
Page, 18
Pamelia, 31
Parlor, 22, 23
Parlour, 24, 40
Patrick, 26
Patsy, 9
Patty, 5, 6, 13, 16, 44
PAYNE: Joseph, 2
Peggy, 1, 12, 13, 16
PELLY: J.B., 37
Pemelia, 32
Pemmy, 41
PENDLETON: Thornton P., 17
PERRY: John, 16
Peter, 12, 14, 16, 21, 36, 38
PETTY: J., 9; John B., 40
Phebe, 16
Phil, 16, 26
Philip, 11, 16, 23, 40
Pierce: Mary, 40
PIERCE: M., 16
Pold, 20
Polk, 15, 20
Polly, 17, 23, 27, 37
POMEROY: Ann, 41
Posey: Charles, 17; George, 24
PRATT: James, 15
Presley, 25
PRICE: Peter, 28
PRIEST: Lewis, 3

Queen, 2, 3, 5, 9, 13, 29

Rachael, 22, 37
Rachel, 1, 2, 6, 13, 31
Ralph, 3, 7, 10, 12, 19, 23, 27,
  29, 32, 34, 37
RANDOLPH: Martha, 2;
  Martha E., 2; Susan B., 3;
  Thomas, 16; Thomas B., 12;
  Thomas Beverly, 2; William,
  7, 10; William May_, 2

Reason, 4, 36, 38
REASON Jr: Anna Case, 12
REASON Sr.: Gerard C.
  Ricketts, 12
Rebecca, 4, 7
REDGEWAY: Harriet, 35;
  William, 35
Reed: Jacob, 38; Jacob H., 34;
  John, 33; John R.C., 34;
  Jonas H., 34, 38; Sarah C.,
  38; Sarah Catharine, 34
REEL: Samuel, 20, 23, 26
Regina, 15, 31
Reuben, 7, 10
Rex, 6
Richard, 1, 2, 13, 17, 20, 21, 23,
  24, 27, 31, 32, 37
RICHARDS: J.R., 29, 43;
  James R., 10, 40, 43; N., 29
RICHARDSON: C., 27;
  Catharine, 5; John C., 42;
  Marcus F., 42; Marcus T.,
  42; Samuel, 5; Samuel C.,
  33, 35, 36, 42; William, 37,
  40, 41
RICKARDS: Cornelius, 37
RICKETT: Elijah, 4
RICKETTS: Elijah, 12;
  Margaret, 12
RIDGEWAY: Harriet, 35;
  Richard, 22, 23, 26; William,
  35
RIDING: Elizabeth E., 4
RILEY: George, 13; Susannah,
  13; William, 10
Rines: Ive, 41
Robbin, 16
Robert, 9, 26, 28, 33, 35, 38,
  39, 44
Roberta, 31
Robin, 19, 24, 33

ROBINSON: Benjamin, 41;
  John, 41; Vincent, 41;
  William, 41
ROBISON: John, 5
ROLLINGS: Sarah, 1
ROWZEE: Morgan, 7; Rachel,
  7
Roxy, 23
ROY: Elijah, 4, 6; Gibson N., 4,
  6
ROZE: G.N., 10
Ruhamah, 23
Russel, 41
Russell, 18
RUST: Bushrod, 32; Charles,
  13; Charles B., 13, 29;
  Elizabeth, 25, 32, 34; John,
  22, 26, 34; John B., 19

Sal, 43
Sall, 8
Sallie, 41
Sally, 3, 6, 8, 9, 11, 12, 15, 25,
  26, 31, 33, 35, 37, 44
Sam, 8, 10, 11, 13, 17, 18, 28,
  32, 35
Samuel, 8, 16, 17, 21, 27
Sandy, 5, 13, 27, 28
Sanford, 3
Sarah, 7, 9, 13, 14, 17, 19, 20,
  21, 22, 23, 25, 27, 28, 29, 31,
  33, 34, 35, 36, 38, 40, 41, 42,
  43
Sary Ellend, 8
Scatta, 42
Sceatta, 35
Sciatta, 29
Scietto, 32
SELF: Henry, 5, 13; John, 5, 9,
  13, 16, 17, 20
SETTLE: Catharine, 27;
  Henrietta T., 27; Vincent, 27,
  28

TRIPLETT: Martha, 11, 13, 16, 19
TROUT: J., 9; Joseph, 20
Turner, 27, 28, 37
TURNER: Robert, 8, 34
TYLER: George, 32; George G., 31, 36, 41

ULAY: Nancy, 19

VANNORT: Alfred, 41, 42; Jacob, 39, 40, 41, 42
Vina, 40, 44

WALKENS: S.P., 35
Walker, 31
WALKER, 35; James W., 17
Wash, 9, 13
Washington, 1, 2, 3, 5, 23, 24
WAY: George, 39; James, 10; Nancy, 10, 31, 34; Robertson, 3, 7, 10, 12
WEIR: James N., 10; James V., 8
Wells: Washington, 39

WELTON: Felix B., 3
Wesley, 38
WHEATLEY: G.T., 25; Manly T., 40
WHEATLY: Ann, 22; George, 22; George T., 24; J.H., 36; James, 22; Mandly, 22; Mary Catharine, 22
WHEELRIGHT: Margaret, 22
WHITE: Ezekiel, 43; Judge, 5; Peggy C., 4
Will, 10, 37, 41
William, 5, 6, 7, 8, 10, 18, 20, 22, 23, 29, 32, 36
William Henry, 18, 23
Willis, 7, 10, 12, 28, 31, 38
Willison, 19
WILSON: Thomas, 21
Winney, 17, 19, 24
WINSBURRY: John W., 29
WOOD: Harrison, 7; Isaiah, 15; Sarah, 7
WOODWARD: Rachal, 39; William, 28, 33

Heritage Books by Sandra Barlau:

Some Slaves of Caroline County, Virginia,
Will Books 19, 29, 30, 31 and 32; and Guardian's Book

Some Slaves of Fauquier County, Virginia
Volume I: Will Books 1–10, 1759–1829
Volume II: Will Books 11–20, 1829–1847
Volume III: Will Books 21–31, 1847–1869
Volume IV: Master Index, Will Books 1–31, 1759–1869

Some Slaves of Frederick County, Virginia, Will Books 1-28, 1743–1868

Some Slaves of Prince William County, Virginia,
Partial Will Books, 1734–1872

Some Slaves of Rappahannock County, Virginia,
Will Books A to D, 1833–1865 and Old Rappahannock County, Virginia,
Will Books 1 and 2, 1664–1682

Some Slaves of Virginia, 1674–1894:
Lost Records Localities Digital Collection of the Library of Virginia

Some Slaves of Virginia:
The Cohabitation Registers of 27 February 1866 from the
Lost Records Localities Digital Collection of the Library of Virginia

Volume I: Augusta County, Buckingham County, Caroline County,
Culpeper County, Floyd County

Volume II: Fluvanna County, Goochland County, Hanover County,
Henry County, Lunenburg County

Volume III: Montgomery County, Prince Edward County, Richmond
County, Roanoke County, Scott County

Volume IV: Smyth County, Surry County, Warren County, Washington
County, Westmoreland County, Wythe County

Volume V: Master Index

Some Slaves of Warren County, Virginia Will Books A, B, C, 1835–1904

Washington, D.C. Slave Owner Petitions, 1862–1863,
Filed under the Act of April 16, 1862 and Other Documents from the
National Archives and Records Administration, Washington D.C.